Taking
Restorative
Justice
to
Schools

A Doorway to Discipline

Jeannette Holtham

TAKING RESTORATIVE JUSTICE TO SCHOOLS
A Doorway to Discipline

Library of Congress Cataloging-in-Publication Data

Holtham, Jeannette
Taking Restorative Justice to schools: A doorway to discipline
ISBN-10: 0-9822706-1-5
ISBN-13: 978-0-9822706-1-5

Visit the Youth Transformation Center online at
www.youthtransformationcenter.org

To order additional copies, or to inquire about bulk orders,
please visit delhayespress.com.

Cover photograph by Stephen Samuel Lemig
Cover design by Jeannette Holtham (Nepalese shawl a gift from
Christopher M. Lemig)

Acknowledgments

Deepest thanks to my loving family for their eternal encouragement and support, especially my sons Christopher and Stephen, my daughter-in-law Mandy, my sister Sandy, my niece Caroline (for countless hours of designing the earlier rendition of this book), my nephew Bob and his wife Nancy, Erik Blake, Carol Kass, Kathy Herron, and Jacqueline Faust. Their remarkable journeys have inspired me to reach beyond my own potential and remain true to myself.

To Andre Zarb-Cousin who set aside his retirement to passionately engage in our trainings and once again make a positive difference in the lives of youth, and to his wonderful family.

To countless friends who have ceaselessly encouraged and advocated for me and for our work with youth, especially Linda Rimer, Debra and Mike Othitis, Steve Elder, Joyce and Steve Schuck, Don Griffin, Pete and Lynn Lee, Rich and Shannon Schur, Rick Rodriguez and Joan Peterson, Greg Snyder (a marketing-storyteller genius), Serena Pearson, Bill Groom, Dr. Jody Glittenberg Hinrichs, Deborah Hendrix, Jim & Marlene Rothwell, Anne Clark, Rebecca Rodriguez, Ken Jaray, Michael Faber, Jan Tanner, Tom Strand, Senator John Morse, Representative Michael Merrifield, Jack Ruszczyk, Karen Lee, Dorcas Wilkinson, Mary Ellen Johnson, Doug Stevenson, Bob Garner, Stacy Dyson, Black Pegasus, Stephen Mack, Richard Randall, Patty Spiers, Dianne Walker, Jeannie Porter, Tom Suddes, Alma Linda Conover, Lori Zimmerman, Maria Flores, and Mike and Cheryl Arrigo.

To former, exceptional students who raised the bar for all others: Amanda McGrath, David Pinnock, Baha Dubose, Tyrone Cox, Shannon Bollenbaugh, Jamie Shull, Jennifer Zentz, Harry "Black" Hammonds, Jr., Trent Phillips, Shamika Jacobs, Ashley Arellanes, and Tamara "Tank" Gary.

To my dear friends Maggie Griggs and Rob Herzfeld for their tireless work keeping up the Youth Transformation Center website; my editor and new friend Jan King Garverick; my long-time friend Clint Hayes, a truly gifted graphic artist and computer wizard, and his wife Carole, whose discerning eyes helped put the final touches on this book; and my publisher Del Hayes, whose impeccable integrity and drive to make a difference in the world helped me over the last hurdle.

And finally, and especially, to God who called me to a higher purpose than my own ego.

Table of Contents

Foreword 1

Introduction 5

1. Applying Restorative Justice to Schools 8
- What Is Restorative Justice, and Why
  Would Schools Want to Use It?
- What Results Are Schools Getting and
  Can We Expect Similar Results?
- What Typical RJ Models Are Schools Using?
- How Much Time Can We Expect to Spend
  Implementing Restorative Justice in Our School?
- What Are the Keys to Success?
- What Can You Expect from This Guide?

2. Make a Plan 18
- Take the First Step
- Gather Your Stats
- Typical School Violations
- How Will You Measure Success?
- Be Prepared to Talk about Cost
- How Do Other Schools Measure Success?
- Create a Simple Mission and Vision Statement
- Ask for Help

3. Prepare Your Boomerang Action Team 27
- Identify Your Team Members
- Tool Number One ~ The Confidentiality Statement
- Tool Number Two ~ The Basic Scripts
- Tool Number Three ~ The Agreement
- Tool Number Four ~ The Written Apology Letter
- Tool Number Five ~ The Consequences
- Tool Number Six ~ Coaching the Community
  Representatives and Supporters
- Reintegrative Shame Versus Stigmatizing Shame

4. Measure, Track, Evaluate 49
  - A Logic Model
  - Collect The Data

5. Connect Your Community with Informal Circles............ 53
  - Not Enough Time
  - The Talking Instrument
  - Check-ins and Check-outs
  - Start of the School Year
  - Circles to Address Behavior Problems
  - Creative Formats for Circles

6. Final Thoughts 66
  - Restorative Justice: A Doorway to Discipline

Appendices

A - Mindset of Those Who Have Been Harmed................. 68

B - Offender Thinking Errors... 70

C - Sample Role Plays.. 72

D - Case Study... 78

E - Needs and Feelings.. 80

F - Additional Ideas for Launching a Restorative Justice
   Initiative.. 83

Foreword

My partner Andre Zarb-Cousin and I recently returned from teaching a restorative justice workshop at the University of Malta. The warm welcome from these people was exceeded only by their genuine interest in restorative justice as a new approach to serving the youth of this densely populated 122 square mile island in the beautiful Mediterranean 120 miles off the boot of Italy.

Dr. Cefai, head of the psychology department at the university and director of the European Centre for Educational Resilience & Socio-Emotional Health coordinated the two-day event that drew an unprecedented 120 educators, counselors, social workers, psychologists, and criminology majors. Typically, he told us, large conferences might draw 15 to 20 or even up to 35 people. He was both amazed and delighted as more and more people registered requiring shifts to larger and larger rooms.

In the four years since this book was originally published, I have been awestruck by three things. From early on I was amazed when I began to get inquiries and book orders from around the world—from countries like Pakistan, India, Australia, New Zealand, Canada, Georgia, Malta, Peru, Kenya, Ireland and the UK along with the U.S. Several university professors inquired about using the book as a text for their students of criminology studies, law, social sciences, and education. The experience in Malta and the growing interest in the book have reinforced for me the historical significance of the restorative justice movement as a pivotal consciousness-raising spreading rapidly across our continents.

Secondly, the burgeoning flow of emails coming in—some curious or wanting clarification about restorative justice principles, some looking to partner with our nonprofit organization Youth Transformation Center —but most, nearly always parents or teachers, desperate for answers as to how to deal with the growing rebellion and violence among youth. I freely share with them some of the tools and insights we've gained in working with troubled youth over the last decade and it gives them a glimmer of hope.

Working at the frontlines of the restorative justice movement has given me the realization that youth are the same everywhere and the challenges we face in helping our children to become responsible, fulfilled adults likewise run parallel. The influences on our young people today are very different than they were a half century ago. Youth are simply responding to the stimuli around them just as our parents and grandparents did to the societal norms of their day.

Why would we expect children to not be impacted and influenced by the intensity of today's Hollywood films filled with violence and graphic sexual content; by violent video games; by cell phones and computer technologies that invite sexting and cyber-bullying? Adolescents typically lack strong social emotional intelligence or the experience to look beyond instant gratification and knee-jerk reactions to potential long-term consequences. We're asking their undeveloped frontal lobes to work overtime to produce thirty year old adults with good decision-making and problem solving skills in thirteen- or seventeen-year-old brains and bodies. Rather than focus on what's missing, however, restorative justice aptly reveals what is inherent in every human being, and that is a sense of right and wrong and a sense of justice. Every one of the more than nine hundred youth we've worked closely with whether we met them after they'd been suspended or expelled from schools or were now in prison knew the difference between right and wrong. And each and every one of them embraced restorative justice as a fair way of dealing with wrongdoing. None of them saw it as an easy way out. This leads me to my third awe-inspiring revelation.

The principles of restorative justice work in nearly all circumstances, even those where RJ is not widely accepted as being appropriate or effective. Some RJ practitioners may read that and catch their breath, aghast at such a bold statement. I hear RJ proponents from around the world who say restorative justice is fine for dealing with behaviors like classroom disruption, interpersonal conflicts, gossip, disrespect of authority, theft, and even simple assault, but you can't use restorative justice for bullying or for sexual assault or for murder. Yet, in these matters the offended parties are in urgent need of healing—a need for which the punitive systems now in place in our courts and schools are unable or unwilling to provide.

It is my sincere belief that we as a human race must rethink our punitive systems that have profited a select group of people who promote adversarial responses to wrongdoing and who typically step in as pseudo victims. I can see Albert Einstein standing right here in front of us saying, "You cannot solve a problem from the same consciousness that created it. You must learn to see the world anew."

Our world is changing by the minute. We must blaze a new trail for our children and grandchildren. We must hold our youth accountable for their behaviors and require that they take a responsible, active role in repairing harm rather than locking them away in a cell or kicking them out of school, only to get behind in their schoolwork (which is now contributing to the accelerating dropout crisis in America as we send an uneducated workforce out into our communities). We can do better.

I am most certainly not suggesting that you read this book and are then ready to facilitate a restorative justice circle dialog between the family of a murdered loved one and the murderer; nor with a family dealing with the horrors of incest or rape. What I am suggesting is that punitive systems are not designed to address the root cause of behavior issues or deal with the wounds of the offended. In simplistic terms they are designed to identify who's to blame and punish those individuals. Restorative justice has proven itself to be effective even in sensitive cases that involve murder and rape. In these cases it works alongside sentencing for the offender while giving victims and families of victims a chance to be heard and a starting point for the long road back to feeling safe and emotionally stable again. It takes a highly experienced restorative justice facilitator to intervene in these cases, but the healing that can and has taken place in countless restorative justice circles where human compassion is present is nothing short of miraculous.

May your own role in this worldwide paradigm shift be truly blessed and inspire others to take the high road along with you.

Jeannette Holtham

Introduction

The year was 1986. After positioning a dummy under the covers of his bunk that passed not one bed check, but two, Richard cut a hole in the fence at the edge of the jail yard, crawled through, shimmied his way to the roof, and lay sideways in the hot sun. Several hours later, with one side of his body badly sunburned, the youth tiptoed to the parking lot, hotwired an old truck, and headed to freedom. Richard had escaped from the "inescapable" Adams County Jail—in broad daylight.

He was serving time for armed robbery. Although he'd only taken $2 from the girls at the shoe store (who testified they weren't really scared of him because he was so nice), Richard then made a bigger haul, $1,200, at the Taco Bell where he'd politely, at gunpoint (albeit unloaded), asked the night manager to open the safe. No one was injured in either of those escapades.

A month after his jail escape, after spending time in the woods behind the campground where his family frequently had gone camping when he was "just a kid," loneliness set in. Heading back to town on foot, desperate to see his family and sleep in a real bed, he stole a van near the airport. Then he stopped to see a "friend" who gave him a gun, and Richard aimed the van toward home—Commerce City, Colorado. The digital clock read close to midnight as he got pulled over for going ten miles over the speed limit.

Panic ripped through Richard's bloodstream as he thought of going back to jail—a place he never wanted to see again. Jamming his foot on the gas pedal, he grabbed the gun and shot out the window. The bullet ricocheted off the van window and lodged in the shoulder of the police officer whose squad car was now in hot pursuit as he opened fire on the back of the van. Richard's arm and hand went numb as a bullet flew through his shoulder and sent blood spurting across the steering wheel and the windshield. Like a fast-action movie it seemed surreal. The gun he threw out the window was never found.

The midnight speed chase was short. Within minutes, several squad cars surrounded the van and eight uniformed police officers on red alert had Richard pinned to the ground. The injured police officer got a purple heart. Seventeen-year-old Richard got ninety-six years.

Two decades later Richard continues to spend 23.5 hours a day in "lock-down" at the Colorado State Penitentiary. If he follows the rules, he might get out of his cell long enough to take a shower or make a brief phone call to his father, who rarely answers any more.

Prison is an unpleasant place at best, a place where incarcerated youth and adults have a lot of time to think. It was intended to be a place where people could cool off and reflect on their wrong doing. A place where they could feel ashamed and guilty, express remorse, and be humbled enough to return to society as civil, obedient citizens. Prison was a place of exile so the community left behind would feel safe. This human experiment has since shown us that locking away select members of our population does not decrease crime or violence; in fact, some believe it increases it.

I visited Richard in prison once a month for nearly five years. I came to know him and his family quite well, particularly his little sister who was dating my younger son for several of those years. During that time their mother died of cancer and Richard made two attempts at escape, stating he'd rather die on the fence than live in prison the rest of his life. I met with the governor's advocate Mark Noel on his behalf during those years to see if the governor would consider reducing or commuting Richard's cruel and unusual sentence. When I related Richard's story to him, he inquired as to whether Richard had gotten a sentence of two years. When I told him it was ninety-six, it jolted him like a thunderbolt. But there was nothing he could do. The governor did not believe in commuting prison sentences.

Richard changed my life. In the few years I knew him I got to see his humbled heart, his hilarious wit, and his brilliantly inventive mind that could have been channeled into far better outcomes. Instead he sits rotting away in a prison cell even today, doing time, a lot of time, and costing you and me $50,000 a year to warehouse, clothe and feed him. When Pell grants for prisoners were taken away, he was not able to finish his associate's degree to keep his mind on learning, and he'd already read most of the books in the sparse library.

I asked myself: What would have happened if someone had cared enough to reach Richard at a core level when he was 12 years of age when he got his first detention for chewing gum in class. What would have happened if someone had taken Richard under their wing when he started skipping school at the age of 16 and gotten him excited about building a robot or exploring a career in engineering, a subject that today fascinates him? And then I asked myself, how many more Richards are out there who are at this very moment at a fork in the road—and the choice they may make tomorrow could cost them their lives.

Because of Richard I answered the call. I'm just an ordinary person, but, like many hundreds of thousands of others around the world, I have joined the worldwide movement referred to as restorative justice. I believe it holds the promise of a new tomorrow for the world around us, especially the Richards who are growing in numbers in schools, in homes, in jails, and even in our faith communities. This book is dedicated to my friend Richard and to all the children whose lives have been or will be transformed through this remarkable technology called restorative justice.

| Chapter 1 |

Applying Restorative Justice to Schools

I watched a bunch of skateboarders the other day at the skate park having a blast fine-tuning their skateboarding prowess. Then I asked them why they weren't in school.

With puffed pride and great glee they retorted, "Oh, we were suspended!"

~ Tim Turley, Restorative Justice Coordinator,
Denver Public Schools

What Is Restorative Justice, and Why Would Schools Want to Use It?

A major shift is taking place around the world as schools come to grips with accelerating issues of student misconduct and alarming media headlines that shout school violence. Like justice systems drowning in case overloads, budget shortfalls, and the high cost of explosive prison-building, educators too are overwhelmed with school closings, reductions in staff, and state and federal mandates that add more responsibility without commensurate financial support. The worldwide movement known as restorative justice holds a key to reducing costs while increasing the safety and well-being of our communities and our schools.

Undeniably, we serve a very different population of youth today than in decades past. Gone are the classrooms where children "toed the line" and where teachers were given carte blanche to discipline with a stick if necessary. Our teachers today need immediate and effective tools to address risky and out-of-control behaviors so they can build stronger school communities and get back to the vital job of teaching. What they don't need is another complex "flavor-of-the-month program" to implement, a high-cost curriculum or license to purchase and annually renew, nor do they need a week-long seminar to attend.

What you will read in these pages is not rocket science. In fact, it is nothing new. I wouldn't even be surprised if you are already using some or all of the ideas you'll find here. If so, great—you're right on time. Read these pages with the comfort of knowing you are aligned with schools around the world that are taking the exciting philosophy known as restorative justice to a whole new level in the 21st century. Why? Because it's simple and it works.

Schools were developed as places of learning, not places where teachers must constantly struggle with problems of misbehavior. Pressured by federal laws that prohibit a one-size-fits-all approach or pointing a finger at poor parenting, developmental/mental illness (i.e., autism, Attention Deficit/Hyperactivity Disorder), or personality traits, schools must now design individualized behavior support strategies. For many educators, using a function-based approach requires taking on new roles and new skills. And as if that weren't enough, time is of the essence. Restorative justice offers an immediate answer to a federally mandated paradigm shift and provides the flexibility to address a wide range of student behaviors and their inherent social and cultural issues.

Howard Zehr, the well-respected pioneer of the modern movement now three decades in existence, aptly reminds us that restorative justice is a philosophy, not a program. That being said, there are specific program models that align perfectly with its philosophy. Other models would more accurately show up on the continuum of offerings in a format referred to as *restorative practices*. In simple terms, restorative justice brings the offender together with his or her victim in a face-to-face gathering that is generally called a *restorative justice conference*—in most models a circle of chairs where there are no physical or emotional barriers between the participants. The dialog encourages each person to talk honestly about what happened, who it affected, and together find a way to repair the harm to the greatest extent possible. The facilitator's job is to remain objective, direct the flow of conversation, and maintain a safe, respectful environment while giving the key stakeholders the power to decide the outcome. The current trend in schools today is to expand that pure restorative justice model by including restorative practices such as informal *circles* that become forums for more general dialog. Included in the final chapters of this book is a model for those circles to give teachers an immediate tool that complement the formal restorative justice process.

In most conventional punitive systems an offender is separated from his or her community—one could even say banished, or ostracized. In the justice system this might be jail time or prison; in the school system, typically detention, suspension or expulsion. With little historical evidence to demonstrate long-term positive outcomes from these isolating responses, many educators have embraced restorative justice with juicy anticipation.

Prior to using restorative practices, the Bessels Leigh School in Oxfordshire, England, experimented with a different method. They believed that increasing punishments would alleviate the accelerating confrontations with students. In fact, it made them worse. After a costly increase in broken windows, the sense of community eroded, and staff-pupil relationships turned to an "us versus them" environment. Soon after taking a restorative justice approach, they found students letting go of their angry and abrasive behaviors and even encouraging their peers to take ownership of their actions.

As a victim-centered process, restorative justice gives the person who has been harmed a chance to be heard, to get vital questions answered, and begin the healing process to feel safe again. It gives the offender a respectful place to be accountable, learn from mistakes, gain empathy for others, and prepare to make better choices in the future. Restorative justice is being used with great success in minor to moderate infractions, misdemeanors, and first-time offenses, and gives offending youth a second chance to wipe the slate clean and start over. In more serious cases, it can complement conventional consequences in order to address the important but often neglected needs of victims.

Restorative justice provides a way to repair the harm of an offense or a crime so that relationships can be restored. It is seen as a way to restore not only the broken relationship between offender and victim, but between offender and community. The conventional system of justice has us view crime as an act against a non-human entity such as a city or state government. In such a system the human victim is set apart from the process and fails to get his/her questions answered. In an unfortunate number of cases the offender is allowed to "plea bargain" to a lesser charge which essentially amounts to a lie—yet another insult to the victim.

Maslow would no doubt say that revenge is not a basic human need; yet, it comes to the fore quite often in conventional responses to crime when the victim's genuine need for safety or connection is unmet. Restorative justice beautifully reminds us that an offense or crime is an act against human beings. When harm is repaired, the community is restored, the victim is empowered, and the offender has a chance to return to his community, with honor, having learned from mistakes and better prepared to take his place as a contributing, conscientious member.

Restorative justice is not "soft on crime" nor is it "touchy-feely" as some fear. I have seen hardened adult criminals buckle at the knees at the very thought of having to face their victim. It's easy to go skateboarding after a suspension, or sit in a jail cell and conjure up the notion you are a "victim" of the system. It is far more difficult to have to listen to how one's behavior has affected others and take an active role in repairing the harm. Victim emotions and offender states of mind commonly rise to the surface during the restorative justice conference along with clues as to the underlying motivations for the offender's behaviors. As the two parties work toward a resolution, transformation becomes possible when the offender shows genuine remorse and gains empathy for those who have been impacted. Underlying issues now can be dealt with honestly, and additional resources can be provided if necessary to address the real concerns and needs of individuals.

As New Zealand criminologist John Braithwaite says (*Crime, Shame and Reintegration*), rather than ask what makes people commit crimes, we should ask, why do most people do the right thing most of the time? The answer of course is simple—connection to community—that same Maslow sense of belonging reinforced in Malcolm Gladwell's *The Tipping Point*. As facilitators of the restorative justice conferences, we have a golden opportunity to nourish our schools with that philosophy. When we ourselves model the behaviors we want to see in our youth such as respect and empathy, it strengthens student-to-teacher and student-to-student relationships. It builds community.

American schools are all too clear about the high cost of a single student being absent on count day. Upwards to six or seven thousand dollars in essential state and federal funding is lost when one student fails to show up at school to be counted. And what about the communities that inherit the youth that has missed so much schoolwork he feels compelled to drop out? The dramatic rise in truancy and dropouts should have all of us concerned. Idle time has a tendency to lead to juvenile crime or to children growing into adulthood without the skills to become contributing members of society and the workforce. Consider the cost to taxpayers when the growing epidemic of generational poverty and an unskilled workforce is ignored. The good news is, challenges such as these have been the catalyst for an unprecedented restorative justice movement that is gaining momentum around the world and now is viewed by many as unstoppable.

Restorative justice is a way to help students process their many social concerns and remove barriers to learning. Empowering youth to make corrections and own their actions is far more powerful than heaping one punishment on top of another.

What Results Are Schools Getting and Can We Expect Similar Results?

Restorative justice complements a school's comprehensive discipline system—it does not replace it. No school using RJ would, or should, purport to its being appropriate for every youth for every offense. Nonetheless, even schools known as the most dangerous and high-risk such as West Philadelphia High School are seeing positive results with restorative justice and its complementary practices. Schools in economically and socially deprived cities are employing restorative justice techniques with marked success. There is no reason to believe, if implemented well, that your school cannot join the growing number of schools in the U.S., the UK, Canada, Australia, New Zealand, and many other countries around the world now experiencing significant reductions in discipline problems and reducing the need for suspension and expulsion. A brief list of schools enjoying these benefits can be found in a later chapter.

Youth take to restorative justice like kites to flying. They are ideal candidates for its benefits. Kids instinctively resonate with the concept of fairness and justice. They know when they've done something wrong even if they feel so squeezed into a corner they make an all-out effort to wiggle their way out through justification, denial, or blame. One of the most brilliant opportunities restorative justice offers is an environment where respect for each person can flourish and where honesty, integrity, and understanding can blossom. And aren't these the very character traits we all want in our children?

The concept of social-emotional intelligence is new ground for our generation. Brilliant visionaries like Daniel Goleman ("Emotional Intelligence" and "Social Intelligence: The New Science of Human Relationships") and George Lucas of *Star Wars* fame (George Lucas Educational Foundation) are catapulting us into a future where social and emotional coping skills will no longer be put on the back burner. Restorative justice and restorative practices can provide a direct conduit to social-emotional skill building and each provides us with compelling, inherent reasons to use it, fine-tune it, and explore new applications to keep up with what's just ahead.

What Typical RJ Models Are Schools Using?

This book provides three simple methods that align with the philosophy of restorative justice and are typical of those being used in many schools around the world. The first is a formal restorative justice "conference" that is popular among many schools for incidents and school violations that harm others and where a formal restorative justice model is needed. The second is a circle process that can be used in classroom discussions to increase connectedness, a simple concept that doesn't require a degree to learn. And third is what I call the boomerang questions, a metaphor for what you give out coming back to you: Anger comes back as anger, respect comes back as respect. These straightforward restorative questions can be placed on bookmarks for all the teachers and staff in your school to use during those "teachable moments" that require an immediate response to classroom disruption, hallway shoving, or school ground fighting; and aren't serious enough to warrant the considerable time investment for a formal RJ conference. School-wide use of these boomerang questions by your entire school staff will begin to turn the tide and plant the seeds for a culture shift that could potentially, and significantly, reduce the number of students being sent to the office. These three approaches used together are simple tools that promote relationship and community building. Inevitably they will find their way outside the school into homes, workplaces, and the community.

How Much Time Can We Expect to Spend Implementing Restorative Justice in Our School?

More than likely your school is currently spending significant time on daily discipline and on suspension and expulsion hearings. Give a rough guess as to how much time your teachers are spending with chronically disruptive, insubordinate, or disengaged students. To produce the kind of results that are possible with restorative justice, your plan deserves some investment of time up front so you can reduce the hours of discipline time down the road. How far down the road? That will depend on how many cases of discipline currently come through your door and how effective your restorative justice implementation is. Many schools are seeing sizable reductions in the first six months. Many of you will hit the ground running after reading this book and will get started the next day putting the process into place and will spoon feed the rest of the school along the way—the one-classroom-at-a-time method. Others of you will be required to convene the larger school community before stepping out which could take weeks or even months to gain consensus or a majority vote. You know the best path to take. This book provides the tools for either route.

What Are the Keys to Success?

One can learn the "mechanics" of a process, memorize each step with perfection, and be able to deliver it almost verbatim. But, courageous educators who have walked this path before you insist it is the three critical elements that follow that will build a strong foundation for success:

- At least one passionate adult advocate from your school with a solid understanding of restorative justice and how it integrates with your overall discipline system. This is the individual who will lead the charge to an eventual whole-school approach where all staff are using the restorative justice language. This does not have to happen overnight. Some schools accomplish this one classroom at a time.
- A simple model such as those presented in this book.
- Facilitators with the right attitude who can remain objective and who will naturally model the behaviors you want to see in all your students (respect, empathy, and genuine concern for others).

Having delivered restorative justice conferences and trainings for many hundreds of youth, teachers, school resource officers, police officers, prison and youth detention center staff, I am consistently reminded that we must all "watch our tone of voice." When a typical youth (or adult for that matter) hears an authoritarian or condescending tone of voice, let's face it, before you can even get the last note out of your mouth, he will be preparing his defense. Next thing you know you're locked into a passive aggressive staring contest or an all-out brawl. Neither will produce the results you're looking for. By contrast, when you approach a youth with genuine interest, concern, and respect, the world of communication opens up and the possibility of transformation rises up to greet you.

Love and Logic, the 75-years-in-the-making philosophy developed for parents and teachers by Jim Fay and Foster W. Cline, M.D. says it this way:

> "Why is it so important to at least look calm and collected as we provide consequences for our children's misbehavior? Because...
> Anger creates resentment and rebellion.
> Empathy ups the odds of genuine remorse and responsibility.
> Anger says, 'I can barely handle you!'
> Empathy communicates, 'I'm such a great parent that I can handle you without breaking a sweat!'
> Anger creates kids who get sneaky and do irresponsible things behind our backs.
> Empathy creates kids who are more likely to behave even when we aren't watching them."

One of my favorite aunts told us her story of "inheriting" a two-year-old son when she married her husband. This child's misbehaviors were more than my young aunt at the age of eighteen could handle. His acts of disrespect and rebellion abruptly turned to defecating in the laundry basket of clean clothes. My aunt was beside herself and finally consulted her physician about how to handle the little tike and still keep her sanity, not to mention her marriage. The wise doctor said, "Until you love the child, nothing will change." She went home in tears and hugged the child who became "her son." She was now able to discipline with love rather than screaming demands. It made all the difference. That boy became one of our favorite cousins, with outstanding social skills and genuine concern for others.

What Can You Expect from This Guide?

A "guide" is precisely that, a template for you to play with, modify, add to and remove elements. It provides you with the flexibility to produce optimum results customized to your particular school environment. I believe that educators have the ideal foundational skills and ability to take the concept of restorative justice and run with it, and I genuinely look forward to seeing how its usage in the school environment will evolve in the coming years through people who believe as I do that our youth deserve every second chance they can get.

This guide is not an encyclopedia of restorative justice. It is for those action-spirited individuals who are ready to take effective action now. It is intended to demystify and simplify the restorative justice concept. I will assume that those of you who wish to do more research will seek out the many excellent academic resources now available on the Web and at your library. I highly recommend four outstanding short, but powerful, reads:

- Macrae, Allan and Howard Zehr. *The Little Book of Family Group Conferences: New Zealand Style.* Intercourse, PA 17534. Good Books. 2004
- Pranis, Kay. *The Little Book of Circle Processes: A New/Old Approach to Peacemaking.* Intercourse, PA 17534. Good Books. 2005
- Stutzman Amstutz, Lorraine and Judy H.Mullet. *The Little Book of Restorative Discipline for Schools: Teaching Responsibility; Creating Caring Climates.* Intercourse, PA 17534. Good Books. 2005
- Zehr, Howard. *The Little Book of Restorative Justice.* Intercourse, PA 17534. Good Books. 2002

Chapter 2

Make a Plan

The new definition of insanity is seeing societal trends as someone else's fault rather than a reflection of ourselves and our attitudes and a golden opportunity to make a difference.

~Anonymous

Take the First Step

You can go in one of two directions for your first step. You can gather a sizable group of key stakeholders from the district, the school, and the community to make a plan, or if you are the primary decision maker, you can jump right into creating your action team in Chapter Three.

If you choose the first option, perhaps because you are in a large district that must get approval from a large body of people, your initial key stakeholder meeting can make the difference in moving forward or stagnating. If you are well prepared and have a solid outline of a plan for them to look at, the individuals around the table will breathe a long sigh of relief that the vision makes sense and some of the planning has already been done for them. Now your job is threefold: to get buy-in from these individuals (even to the point of letting them think it's their idea); to set your measurements in place so you will know how to define success; and lastly, to mobilize your boomerang action team that will facilitate and track the actual restorative justice cases.

As you may have guessed, knowing your key stakeholders well and how they might respond to the opportunity is critical. Only you can do that. You're the one who picked up this book, so the Universe has chosen you as the right person to drive this mission forward. You now can talk with each individual casually beforehand and feel them out on their understanding of the school's needs and the possible opportunity restorative justice offers. Or, you can set up a "mystery" meeting where all are invited to explore a new idea or address school discipline challenges. Then again, you can run the other way. I have a feeling you'll jump right in and be seen as a brilliant leader who produces results.

Here is a list of decision makers and implementers that many schools, particularly those in large metro areas, may want at the table. It's up to you how many and who to invite. Ask yourself who will fund the initiative, who will advocate for it, and who will implement.

- School board members
- Superintendent
- Principal
- Vice Principal
- Counselors and behavior support personnel
- Teachers
- Select students
- Parents, PTA/PTO members
- School Resource Officers
- Chief of Police or SRO Supervisor
- Community members
- Business leaders (Community support can be a tremendous boost to your school and provide opportunities for future recognition and resources such as potential sponsorships and important advocacy.)
- Juvenile magistrate or judge

Gather Your Stats

Once you've decided on who your key stakeholders are, you will set a meeting date and location. Together you will make a plan. Now let's get prepared for that initial gathering. Select some basic stats that show the school's need. Here is a sample chart:

	Total Count	Male	Female	White	Black	Hisp	Asian	Am Indian	Other
Total school population									
Number of school detentions per 100 students									
Number of in-school suspensions per 100 students									
Number of out-of-school suspensions per 100 students									
Number of expulsions per 100 students									
Number of law enforcement referrals per 100 students									
Number of excused absences									
Number of unexcused absences									
Number of truancies									
Number of absences specifically on count day/week									
Graduation rate									
Academic improvement									

Typical School Violations

Have a list of school violations ready for the team to discuss. In a phased-in approach, you might consider referring only specific minor violations to the restorative justice conference model; and once your team has gained some experience, you can then include more serious incidents. Here is a comprehensive list of violations most schools deal with these days:

Assault (1st or 2nd degree)	Nuisance Activity
Attendance policy violation	Out-of-Class Disruption of Learning Environment
Bullying	Possession or Use of Legal Drugs
Bus Misconduct	Profanity
Crime of Violence	Robbery
Defiance of Authority	Sexual Harassment
Disrespect of Peers	Sexually Explicit/Indecent Behavior
Disrespect of Staff	Smoking/Tobacco
Dress Code Violation	Student Conflict (Non-Physical), Verbal
Ethnic and Racial Slurs	Student Conflict (Physical)
Felony	Tardiness
Fighting (3rd Degree)	Theft
Gang Related Activity	Threats Against Peers
Habitually Disruptive	Threats Against Staff
Harassment	Truancy
In Class Disruption of the Learning Environment	Use Possession Sale or Distribution of Alcohol or Illegal Drugs
Internet Harassment	Vandalism
Lying/False Information	Weapons

How Will You Measure Success?

Your school's statistics are the perfect starting place for determining your goals. Decide what to tackle first. Is your primary aim to reduce suspensions and expulsions? Do you want to target chronically disruptive students or perhaps the chronically tardy? Is it more important to address the needs of those most at risk of dropping out? Some schools have an immediate need to deal with insubordinate youth that have accosted teachers and staff. Specific violations such as interpersonal conflicts, fighting, and bullying are typically good places to start. It's up to you to determine highest priorities.

How accurate and how user friendly is your data collection software? Whether you use someone on the school staff or an outside evaluation firm, the data you collect will be invaluable to the program's sustainability. An independent evaluator can objectively analyze your data and help you see where the program has had impact, where it can be improved, and, ultimately, how it can be self-sustaining. Extensive outside evaluations could run in the vicinity of $17,000. If you apply for an implementation grant, a formal evaluation may, in fact, be required, and the cost of the evaluation can be included in the grant request. Outside objective evaluations are well worth the dollars spent as they justify future grant or other funding opportunities.

What is the value of a school shifting its paradigm so that it gains state and national recognition as a top performing academic learning environment rather than a school plagued with discipline problems and in danger of being closed? Can we really put a price tag on that?

Be Prepared to Talk about Cost

Budgets have become critical issues for schools. Take a look at the cost of your school's current discipline system; the cost for dedicated staff and teachers that must deal with students whose behaviors challenge school policies and jeopardize the safety and well-being of the entire school community. Assess your results honestly. Are there students still re-offending even after codified measures are taken? There is a cost in human capital that goes far beyond financial. It includes teacher burnout and turnover as well as students unprepared for life. As the world raises its "green" consciousness, we should consider the human capital that is wasted when we lose students or the priceless gift of talented teachers. As of this writing, the City of Hull, one of England's most economically and socially deprived cities having schools with the lowest ranking overall received the highest ranking of "Outstanding" after using restorative practices for just two years; and, in the process, they reduced staff absences from 1380 to 517.

Now let's look at the possible hard costs of implementation. If your school staff is maxed out emotionally and on curriculum delivery overload but has access to funding, you can choose to bring in an experienced restorative justice coordinator to conduct, monitor, and track each restorative justice conference. If funds are tight but you have the time and energy to invest up front and want to lead the charge, you can take the do-it-ourselves approach using this book as your trainer. Here is a sample comparison of costs:

	Additional Outside Consultant	In-House Staff
RJ coordinator (facilitates, tracks, and reports back)	$35,000 to $40,000 annual salary plus benefits	$_____ current salary provided by school or district
Printed materials	$2,500	$_____
Evaluation	$17,000	$_____ in-house data collection

Create your own best guess cost sheet and be certain the team is still on board with you after discussing financial considerations. If there still are concerns about cost, suggest they get creative about additional sources of funding (i.e., school board or superintendent's contingency fund, state or federal grants, local business sponsorships, individual donations from community, school alumni, PTA/PTO fundraiser, or a student fundraiser such as a car wash or obstacle race). Remove the funding barriers. The return on investment is well worth it!

Here are a few thoughts from your peers to address the ongoing debate as to whether it is better to have an in-house restorative justice coordinator or hire an outside specialist:

In-house: Through the leadership of a single passionate in-house advocate (or team) all staff will begin to use the language and the concept. The restorative justice philosophy then stands a better chance of becoming imbedded in the school's culture; and teachers will carry the circle concept into their classrooms to reduce the number of office referrals. If an outside experienced RJ facilitator doesn't exist in the community that can be hired, then in-house staff must get trained or train themselves.

Outside specialist: This approach takes the burden off of staff. Unlike counselors or school administrators who wear multiple hats, an outside consultant is specialized in restorative justice and is not sidetracked or diverted from their focus. Particularly in the initial launch, an outside consultant brings a fresh look at the school's challenges.

If self-sustainability is your school's primary goal, then promoting in-house facilitation as quickly as possible is the best approach. If, on the other hand, in-house facilitators would have considerable biases toward students, particularly repeat offenders, then an outside, objective consultant may better handle the initial start-up phase. An effective restorative justice facilitator must remain impartial so that offending students can trust that they will be heard, and consequently, will be better able to listen.

How Do Other Schools Measure Success?

Below is a short list of schools you may want to contact that are significantly reducing discipline problems and the need for suspensions and expulsions through the use of restorative justice.

- Numerous schools in Pennsylvania, Canada and Britain. The report, *Improving School Climate: Findings From Schools Implementing Restorative Practices,* is available online at: www.iirp.org.

- Denver Public Schools, Denver, CO. Contact Restorative Justice Coordinator Tim Turley (timothy_turley@dpsk12.org) or Ben Cairns (benjamin_cairns@dpsk12.org) for the latest executive summary.
- Manitou Springs Middle School, Manitou Springs, CO. Contact School Counselor Serena Pearson at: spearson@mssd14.org
- University of Colorado at Boulder, CO. Contact Jamal K. Ward, Director, at jamal.ward@colorado.edu
- Drayton School near Banbury, England. Contact Harriet Wall. View video at www.teachers.tv/video/1510
- Rozelle Public School, Sydney, New South Wales, Australia. Contact Lyn Doppler or Lesley Oliver. See www.safersanerschools.org/library/australia.html
- Poudre School District, Ft. Collins, CO. Contact Teri Ashley, Fourth Grade Teacher, at tashley@psdschools.org
- Centre for Restorative Justice, Adelaide, Australia. Contact Leigh Garrett at lgarrett@oars.org.au

Create a Simple Mission and Vision Statement

Sample Vision: "[Name of your school] will resolve incidents of harm to individuals and property in a respectful, safe and restorative manner."

Sample Mission: "To promote the use of restorative justice principles and practices wherever appropriate at [name of your school]."

Consider having your student restorative justice team create posters announcing the vision and mission statements. Or you could run a creative poster contest for the entire student body declaring the school a restorative justice community.

Ask for Help

It is always so revealing to find that many of the youth we work with suddenly realize they can ask for help. Many of us, even as adults, need to re-learn that lesson as well. If people are given a chance to support us, it strengthens relationships, builds community, and creates a result that is far more powerful than if we were to do it all ourselves. Include as many enthusiastic people as you can in this important effort to increase the energy and excitement of launching your restorative justice initiative. Your open and inspiring leadership will offer people the chance to make a meaningful contribution. Here are some ideas:

- Learn the three "Boomerang Bookmark" questions and use them whenever possible in those on-the-spot teaching moments, whether at home, at the office, at school, or at your faith community (see Appendix G). Print out as many bookmarks as you need for school staff including teachers, janitors, secretaries, and para-professionals.
- Start a waiting list for those who wish to serve as community members in an upcoming formal restorative justice conference.
- Get trained and join the boomerang action team that will, in turn, train students or will themselves facilitate the formal restorative justice conferences.
- Ask someone in the group or a business sponsor to buy *Taking Restorative Justice to Schools: A Doorway to Discipline* to distribute to interested teachers who will use the principles directly in their classrooms.

Chapter 3

Prepare Your
Boomerang Action Team

"We tried a [restorative justice] conference with one of the most 'hard-core' girls in the school who 'was in tears within minutes' after having the opportunity to tell her story, as well as hear how her behavior affected others. She has been much better behaved since."

~ Stephen J. Rodriguez, Principal
Pottstown High School, Pennsylvania

Identify Your Team Members

Like a boomerang, what goes out must come back. Anger comes back as anger. Respect comes back as respect. Your core action team is key to the success of your restorative justice initiative. Through their own attitudes and behaviors, your team will convey this profound boomerang metaphor. You must identify a committed and reliable group of individuals that will hold offenders accountable for harmful behaviors while maintaining a persona of openness and respect. They will be the individuals that will execute the process, monitor progress, and assess results. Who and how many will you need? Some schools recommend:

REFERRER: Someone who will refer cases (i.e., school counselor, principal, discipline director, school resource officer).

ADVISOR(S): One to three adult advisors who will co-facilitate the restorative justice conferences and train and monitor the student facilitators and participants.

FACILITATORS: Five to seven (high school or middle school) students who will facilitate. Once in place and working smoothly at the middle and high school levels, consider sending these same students to train staff and students at the elementary feeder schools—a great way to enhance and reinforce their own skills and leadership strengths. Be sure to consider former offending students that have walked in the shoes of any new offenders. They can play a tremendous role in creating a culture shift when their visible behaviors are transformed to show positive peer role modeling.

VOLUNTEERS: Volunteer community members (i.e., parents, business leaders, coaches, janitors, teachers, etc. who may wish to sit in to represent the community when called upon). Restorative justice is a powerful way to re-engage parents and the community in the success of your school.

Now gather the essential tools that follow to assist your boomerang action team in producing optimum results.

Tool Number One ~ The Confidentiality Statement

Although optional, having people sign a confidentiality statement at the start of a restorative justice dialog circle reinforces the concept of "what's said in this room stays in this room and should not be a subject of gossip." It serves

---

SAMPLE CONFIDENTIALITY AGREEMENT

We understand and agree that everything said during the restorative justice conference is confidential. (There are two exceptions—allegations of child abuse and/or neglect, or a threat of future harm.)

We also understand that we may have certain legal rights under the law and, if any of us would like them explained, we will seek legal advice.

_____   _____
Signed   Date

_____   _____
Signed   Date

as an important reminder that human lives deserve trust and respect; and it honors those that have made mistakes, giving them space to learn and grow and make better choices in the future. School communities, just like any other community group, can be hotbeds of rumor and gossip. The more we foster a high expectation for respect and confidentiality, the more integrity we'll instill in ourselves and in our children as they grow into adulthood.

Tool Number Two ~ The Basic Scripts

What does McDonalds have in common with restorative justice? It can be run by teenagers. All it takes is following well-articulated instructions and using the right tools. French fries come out of fryers perfect every time because the fryer is set at a certain temperature and a bell goes off when they're done. I'm not suggesting that the CEO and all the franchise owners give up their status and make way for a teen takeover. Neither am I suggesting that launching a restorative justice initiative in schools should be overseen by youth.

What I am excited to report, however, is that when given the user-friendly tools that are included in the following pages, teens can become leaders who, in turn, influence their fellow students and hold them accountable for behaviors that inevitably impact the entire school community. In the process, they reinforce for themselves important lessons that can be taken into adulthood to serve the wellbeing of their own families and future generations. Once again, students should not be selected only from the student council or yearbook staff or MVP lists, but from former offenders who, because of their own mistakes, may have a greater impact on others—many for whom this could be the first real opportunity to be seen as positive leaders—a life-changing win-win for everyone.

After you've received a case referral and made separate phone calls first to the person that has caused harm ("offender") and then to the person harmed ("victim"), you will meet with each one of them in person. Feel free to customize the following three scripts to suit the age, maturity, and personality of each student, as well as the nature of the offense, and the willingness of the individuals to participate. When a formal restorative justice conference is required, much of the work takes place in the pre-conference with offender and victim. It is here where the facilitator gains the trust so essential to a good conference. It is here where you lay the groundwork through developing a rapport with each party and clearly set expectations so that each feels safe and ready to proceed.

(NOTE: It is not necessary for your student facilitator to memorize the scripts. It is perfectly acceptable to read the scripts during a conference so that no important details are missed. Also, although the terms "offender" and "victim" are not ideal words, they do allow us to distinguish between the parties. Avoid using them as labels for individuals. It is preferable to simply address people by their names in the conference and pre-conference. Other terms such as "the person who caused harm and the person who was harmed" get the point across, but are lengthy for repetitive references. The judicial system has devised many terms such as "defendant" or "accused.")

Script #1: Offender Pre-Conference

Hello [offender's name]. Thanks for coming. I'm [your name]. Your case was referred to me by [individual or agency] in order to help you find a way to repair the harm you caused on [date] when you [describe offense]. We use what is called a restorative justice conference for incidents like these. I'm going to explain the process and help you to make a decision as to whether you would like to participate. But first, why don't you tell me in your own words what happened that day. [Now ask additional clarification questions that help you as the facilitator to gain a clear understanding of what happened while gaining rapport with the offender(s).]

Can you tell me what you were thinking about at the time? Who do you think was affected by your actions and how do you think they were affected? *[Or,* How do you suppose *[name of victim]* is feeling about all this?*]*

If you had it to do over again, *[name of offender]*, what would you do differently? *[Or,* Do you feel now that you had other options at the time that may have resulted in a more positive outcome?*]*

What do you think would be the best possible outcome from this restorative justice conference gathering? *[Or,* How would you like to see things turn out?*]*

Now I'm going to give you an idea of what the restorative justice conference will look like. Now that I've met with you, I'll meet with the person that has been harmed. Then, as long as you and they agree to come together to find a way to repair the harm, I'll set a meeting date and let you know when and where it will take place. At the restorative justice conference we'll sit in a circle facing one another to discuss what happened. I'll ask some questions and give everyone a chance to answer. You will have the opportunity to invite people to that meeting who will support you.

I am there to support both you and the person who was harmed, and to be sure everyone is showing respect for one another. Your job will be to talk about what happened just like you've done with me today, and then to listen to what the others have to say about how your behavior affected them. So, this is a chance for you to learn—in a safe environment—how the incident affected others. Then, we'll all brainstorm and come up with ways to repair the harm. *[Name]*, I want to be sure you understand that it is your behavior that is at issue, not you as a person. And we all can change our behaviors.

[Note: If the offender has minimized his/her responsibility, you might say: I want to be sure that this conference goes well for you. I hear you

describing what happened. You've admitted that you did it, but you also seem to be blaming others (*or* "...to be minimizing your own behaviors"). That might make everyone angry with you. Perhaps there are some reasons why things happened the way they did, but it might be best if you just took responsibility for what you did right up front. We can't control what others do. We can only control what we ourselves do. So, when a person is really honest and sincere and admits what they did wrong without any justifying or making excuses, things go a whole lot better. Do you understand? Why don't you try it again. Just say what you did, and take responsibility for that. (*Acknowledge the student if he has revised his statement successfully.*)]

So, what do you think? Is the restorative justice conference something you'd like to participate in? You realize that if you choose not to, you will have to report back to [*referring person or agency*] and have to deal with the regular consequences [*such as suspension, expulsion, or law enforcement intervention*].

Who would you like to have with you at the restorative justice conference to support you? Is there someone who knows you well and cares a great deal about you, and that you care about? A parent, brothers or sisters, a coach, a teacher, a friend? Maybe a priest, or rabbi, or a neighbor? [*Write down names and contact phone numbers.*] Would you like to call and invite them, or would you rather I did?

I'm going to meet with [*name of victim(s)*] next, and then I'll set a date for our restorative justice conference. I'll let you know the date and time and location. Will you be able to get to that meeting on time with your supporters? Will you need transportation to get there?

Do you have any other questions? Please don't hesitate to call me if you have any questions at all.

And do I have the best phone number(s) to reach you in case something comes up? I'm very pleased that you want to proceed with the restorative justice conference. I'm confident that you will do well.

Having gotten the offender's voluntary consent to proceed, you now can meet with the victim. Meeting first with the offender is important as it allows you to reduce the victim's fear and anxiety when you can announce that the offender is willing to participate to repair the harm. There are subtle and intentional differences in the offender and victim pre-conference scripts to allow you to express empathy to the victim and hold the offender to task. Your sincere empathy will reassure the victim you plan to do everything you can to ensure their safety in the restorative justice conference. Part of your job as the facilitator is to encourage the victim to participate so he or she can reap the benefits of the process (i.e., get essential questions answered; be able to tell the offender how the incident has impacted his/her life; have a say in consequences, and play a significant role in helping the offender to make better choices in the future). Be sure to train your student facilitators in the victim and offender mindset lists found in Appendix A and B.

Script #2 Victim Pre-Conference

Hello [*victim's name*]. Thanks for coming. I'm [*your name*]. Your case was referred to me by [*individual or agency*]. I understand that there has been an incident on [*date*] when [*name of offender*], [*describe offense*]. I'm so sorry that you were harmed by his/her behavior. We'd like to use what is called a restorative justice conference to give you a chance to tell [*name of offender*] how his/her actions have affected you, and give him/her a chance to repair that harm. My job is to make sure you are safe, and make sure you have a say in how that harm will be repaired. I'm going to explain the process for you in just a minute and help you decide whether you would like to participate. But first, why don't you tell me in your own words what happened that day? [*Add any clarification questions that will help you as the facilitator gain a clear understanding of what happened while gaining rapport with the victim(s).*]

Can you tell me what you were thinking about at the time?

How did all this affect you? [*Look for physical, emotional, mental, and financial harms.*]

Who besides yourself do you think was affected and how do you think they were affected?

What do you think would be the best possible outcome from this restorative justice conference gathering? [*Or,* What would you like to see *(name of offender)* do to repair the harm and help you to feel safe again? *Or,* How would you like to see things turn out? *If the victim(s) cannot answer this question right now, encourage him/her/them to think about that before the conference gathering.*]

Now I'm going to give you an idea of what the restorative justice conference will look like. I've met with [*offender's name*]. He has taken responsibility for his actions and said he is willing to come together and hear what you have to say and work on repairing the harm. We'll sit in a circle to have that discussion. I want you to be able to invite people to that meeting who will support you. Is there someone you can think of that you'd like to be there (parent, friend, coach, teacher, priest, rabbi, etc.)? Each person in the circle will be given an opportunity to speak in his/her turn. The benefit to you is that you'll get questions answered and have a say in [*name of offender*]'s consequences. You'll also be helping [*name of offender*] to make better choices in the future.

My job will be to ask the questions and make sure everyone is safe and being respectful. Your job will be to talk about what happened just like you've done with me today, and then to listen to what the others have to say about the incident.

So, what do you think? Is the restorative justice conference something you'd like to participate in? [If the victim(s) chooses not to participate, ask him/her if they'd like someone to stand in for them, generally referred to as a "victim advocate." This person would then speak on their behalf and ensure that the offender is kept accountable and will have a say in how the harm will be repaired.]

Would you like me to call your supporters and invite them, or would you like to take care of that?

I'll arrange for our restorative justice conference and I'll let you know the date and time and location. Will you be able to get to that meeting on time with your supporters? Will you need transportation to get there?

Do you have any other questions? Please don't hesitate to call me if you have any questions at all. And do I have the best phone number(s) to reach you in case something comes up? I'm very pleased that you want to proceed with the restorative justice conference. Again, I'm so sorry that you've had to deal with this, but I'm confident that together we can make things a lot better for you by doing this. Thank you for helping us to make our school community safer.

Now that you've met with each of the separate parties and are ready to move forward, here is the basic script for the formal restorative justice conference for your facilitators.

Remember, it's up to the facilitator to set an objective tone of respect and fairness to all. It is not your place to be judgmental or determine the outcome. Especially remember: watch your tone of voice.

Script #3: Restorative Justice Conference

Welcome. My name is [your name], and I will be facilitating this conference. [Introduce co-

facilitator, if any.] Let's go around the circle now and have each person introduce him or herself.

Thank you all for attending. I know this is difficult for all of you, but your presence will help us deal with the matter that has brought us together. This is an opportunity for all of you to be involved in repairing the harm that has been done and help to make our school community a safer place for all of us.

This conference will focus on an incident which occurred [*state the date, place and nature of offense without details*]. It is important to understand that we will focus on what [*offender name(s)*] did and how that behavior has affected others. This is not an opportunity to blame or shame anyone. This conference is not about punishment. We are only interested in understanding what happened, and determining how to repair harms and impacts, so that [*name of offender(s)*] can make better choices in the future.

We have only a few guidelines: Everyone must speak openly and honestly. Please do not interrupt the person speaking. And all members of the conference must commit to keeping the discussion confidential. Can everyone agree to that? [*Wait for agreement, and have each person now sign the confidentiality agreement.*]

We will have three rounds of questions and discussion, and everyone will have the opportunity to speak.

ROUND ONE:

First we'll talk about <u>what happened</u>. Who would like to begin? [*Give preference to the victim if he/she is present. Ask other participants if they have clarification questions about what happened.*]

[*Consider additional questions such as: Would this have happened if alcohol wasn't involved, or if you'd had less to drink? What time of day did you say it was? Was this the first time anyone said such a thing to you? Was there something going on in your life that made things worse? What were some other options you had that day/evening? Who did you say was with you? Be certain everyone in the circle has had a chance to speak and have their questions answered before moving to Round Two.]*

ROUND TWO:

We'll now move to round two where we'll identify harms and impacts. <u>Who was harmed? And how were they harmed</u>? *[Open this up to anyone who would like to begin, giving preference again to the victim. During this round of questions be sure the group has considered all the possible indirect victims such as: parents, siblings, the school resource officers, police officers who responded to the scene, neighbors, passers-by, roommates, fellow students, teachers, etc. You might ask each person in the circle: How has it affected you? Has it affected your health, your schoolwork, or your desire to attend school? Ask offender, How might you have felt if this had happened to you? Be certain everyone has had an opportunity to speak before moving to Round Three.]*

ROUND THREE:

<u>What can be done to repair the harm</u>? Who would like to begin? *[Collect ideas with no judgment during the discussion until all ideas are out. The "consequences" written into the Agreement must be specific, achievable, measurable, and relevant to the incident. Ask the offender which of these ideas seems do-able in the required timeframe. Determine which he or she will comply with and be successful at. You want a win-win for all key stakeholders.*

SAMPLE AGREEMENT

This Agreement is a sincere effort to repair the harm caused by a specific incident and intended to make amends to the school and community. If this Agreement is not fulfilled, or not fulfilled on time, the case may be referred back to the originating person or agency for appropriate legal or other consequences.

Name of person that caused harm ("offender"):	
Name of person that caused harm ("offender"):	
Name of person that was harmed ("victim"):	
Name of person that was harmed ("victim"):	
Date of incident:	
Nature of incident:	
Name of person that referred the case:	
Names of facilitator and co-facilitator:	
Date of restorative justice conference:	
Conditions of Agreement	

Verbal apology required	Yes or No
Written apology required	Yes or No
Financial reparation required?	How much? $
Required completion date:	
How the harm will be repaired to the victim(s):	1. 2. 3.
How the harm will be repaired to the community:	1. 2. 3.

Signatures

I agree to the conditions set forth above.

Offender:	Offender:
Victim:	Victim:
Witness:	Witness:

Final Report [Provide notes about whether the Agreement was fulfilled on time and to the satisfaction of the parties; what attitudes and actions made the restorative justice conference successful (or not); anything said or done that could have resulted in a better outcome; or, what can be expected from the parties in the future. The report should be submitted to the originating source of referral upon fulfillment of the Agreement.]

Have the co-facilitator recap the recommended repairs for the Agreement. Ideally, get consensus. Be certain everyone has had a chance to speak and give their input. Write up the Agreement and have each of the parties sign it.]

A copy of the Agreement will be given to *[offender's name and victim's name]. All items must be completed by [date must be prior to any return court hearing date or referral agency return date, usually 30, 60 or 90 days after the date of referral depending on the severity of the offence and the expected time required for the repairs]. [Hand out evaluations to all participants for their completion.]*

Tool Number Three ~ The Agreement

Three individuals (or groups/parties) will determine the best way to repair the harm: the offender and his or her supporters, the victim and his or her supporters, and the community member(s) present at the conference. The Agreement should be in writing and signed by each of those individuals or groups of individuals. The facilitator will follow up to be certain the offender has completed the agreed upon action items—on time—and to the satisfaction of those who have been harmed. Leave some space at the end of the Agreement to report back on results to the originating source (i.e., the person who referred the case, such as the school counselor or school resource officer).

Tool Number Four ~ The Written Apology Letter

Here are some simple guidelines for a written letter of apology: Minimum of one written page. Describe the incident and what you were thinking about when you committed the offense. How do you think your behavior has affected the victim? Make a sincere apology. What would you do differently if put in the same position again? What have you done since the offense or what are you going to do to show that you regret your actions and are taking steps to repair the harm?

If you feel it's appropriate, you can take the concept of the written apology letter into a preliminary reflection paper for offending students to fill out prior to the pre-conference. This works particularly well with repeat offenders that have become used to the attention their negative behaviors bring, or who are looking forward to a short vacation (i.e., suspension). It also works well with mutual offenders, in other words, in incidents where both parties are offenders and both are victims (which is quite common in cases of fist fighting or interpersonal conflicts). It helps to flesh out the "who did it first" syndrome while getting youth to focus on their own behaviors and reactions rather than blaming others.

A reflection paper can interrupt chronic behavior patterns and give a student the chance to look at underlying issues and impact. For example, a student that repeatedly disrupts class just before a test because it's preferable to get thrown out rather than be embarrassed at failing the test or being found out for not understanding the work can be helped to see that asking for help is a much more beneficial response. Here is a generic reflection paper questionnaire:

- What happened?
- Who did it affect?
- How did it affect me and the others?
- What was going on just before the incident happened?
- What was I thinking just before and during the time of the incident?
- Why do I think I behaved the way that I did?
- Did I feel a loss of power before or during the incident?
- What do I lose out on when something like this happens?
- If I had it to do over again, what would I do differently?

Tool Number Five ~ The Consequences

It never ceases to amaze me when groups involved in the restorative justice dialog come up with profoundly creative and effective consequences for the actions and behaviors that have harmed their communities. Youth many times can invent relevant and appropriate consequences that adults would never have imagined. Oftentimes, just having an offender sit with his or her peers and have to be accountable can turn a life around. Nonetheless, the group must be ready to provide recommendations that can be discussed and settled on in order to create a positive outcome.

So how do we provide consequences that are relevant to the offense, measurable (with a set date for completion), specific rather than vague, and achievable by the offender(s)? If a youth slashes someone's tire, buying a new car for the victim is not a fair or just consequence. Purchasing a new tire would be appropriate and relevant. You would know when it was accomplished. A timeframe for completion could be built around how much time it will take the youth to earn enough money to pay for the tire, let's say thirty to sixty days. Now it's measurable by time as well. We know what specific and relevant action will be taken in what period of time. Is it achievable? A tenth grader would be more likely to pay for a tire than would a fourth grader.

Those in the restorative justice dialog circle must decide whether the youth can come through on his or her promise and commitment. In the case of a younger student, a parent could provide immediate restitution, but the facilitator might encourage the parent to find a way for the youth to pay back the financial help. Selling some toys could give a younger offender a way to pay restitution and ensure they have some "skin in the game"—an incentive to not re-offend. Once in writing, the Agreement should not be changed.

It is often difficult for many individuals who have used punitive consequences for many years to make the shift to restorative solutions. They somehow believe that students will become more aggressive or more violent if they are not severely punished. Although they are in the minority, I have seen even school resource officers make statements such as, "Throw 'em out of school. Get rid of the trouble makers." When further questioned about what happens after a student is "thrown out," the typical reply is, "They head over to the park across the street. Then the police officers at the park have to deal with them. It's no longer our problem." It is not uncommon, and can, in fact, be quite amusing, to discover during yet a little more inquiry that these same school police officers were "trouble makers" when young and report that they got many second chances. If faced with a difficult staff member or SRO who exhibits a similar attitude, it's best to help him or her keep an open mind and reserve judgment until the restorative justice pilot project shows positive results.

Now let's compare a punitive with a restorative solution. Let's say a tenth grader shoved a ninth grader in the hall and called him a derogatory name. A punitive response would put the tenth grader in detention "to cool off." The younger ninth grader would return to class but with less surety about whether he would be safe from a future encounter, perhaps even planning revenge (because his basic need for safety had not been met). The tenth grader would sit in detention perhaps doing his homework, or just doodling, but more than likely not considering the harm done to the other person or seeking ways to repair that harm.

By comparison, a restorative solution would require that the tenth grader take responsibility for his behavior, volunteer to participate in a restorative justice dialog, and listen to, and truly hear, the ninth grader tell of the impact the incident had on him. The tenth grader might actually be moved by the ninth grader's account and begin to recognize the impact his actions have on others. By not providing that opportunity, we keep our children from gaining important insights into social skills that are vital to their success as adults.

The chart on the following pages illustrates some punitive and restorative responses for comparison.

Tool Number Six ~
Coaching the Community Representatives and Supporters

Community representatives are an important link in the circle. More often than not their lives are changed for the better as they participate in the restorative justice dialog. Be sure to invite students, teachers, administrators, parents, business leaders, and neighbors of the school to sit in on these formal conferences whenever you feel they can make an important contribution to the experience.

INFRACTION	PUNITIVE	RESTORATIVE
Graffiti or property damage	Get referred to law enforcement. Pay a court fee or fine.	Help clean, repair, or repaint, and pay for damages.
Putdowns, gossip, or interpersonal conflicts	Spend time in detention.	Write a letter of apology to the individual(s) harmed; write a reflection paper on how it feels to be put down or gossiped about.
Classroom disruption	Be shamed in front of the class by the teacher.	Verbally apologize to the teacher and fellow students with a promise to contribute more positively in the future. Request that peers hold him/her accountable. Spend a week assisting the teacher with classroom supervision or clean-up.
Bullying younger students	Sent to in-school suspension; have privileges removed.	Set up a weekly book reading with the younger students and read to them out of *Touching Spirit Bear*, a book about restorative justice that addresses a serious assault. Facilitate a circle with individuals considered bullies and discover three reasons why they do it. Facilitate a circle with victims of bullies and find out how bullying affects others.
Ridicule or racial slurs of another individual or group	Given a sanction to stay away from the person in the future.	Participate in a blanket drive for the homeless. Help on a project to raise community awareness to stop "hate crimes." Set up a panel of speakers who can talk to the entire class or school about intolerance and the effect it has on our communities. Write a letter of apology to the person harmed and his/her family. Attend three different faith community youth groups.

Fighting	Sent on out-of-school suspension.	Prepare and deliver a speech to a classroom or larger school assembly about how to negotiate with words rather than fists. Teach a class during detention on anger management and self-control. Read the book *Boundaries for Kids* and give an oral report on it.
Theft	Sent on out-of-school suspension.	Return the stolen items with a sincere verbal or written apology. Pay for replacement of stolen items.
Use and possession of drugs	Expelled from school.	Do community service in a drug rehab center or hospital where addicts are being treated. Spend a night under supervision in a rehab center.
Internet harassment	Sent on out-of-school suspension.	Contribute to a school newsletter article on how Internet harassment damages individual relationships. Write a research paper on recent Internet harassment incidents that have resulted in emotional depression or suicide of the person who was harmed.
Unintentional arson or property damage	Suspension or expulsion	Ride along with fire fighters. Visit a fire station. Interview paramedics.
Truancy	Get referred to law enforcement.	Write a reflection paper on assets for youth. Help facilitate a circle discussion on truancy and identify why some kids skip school. Interview a recent high school graduate that dropped out of school and returned after recognizing the value of a high school diploma. Interview a college student and ask why he or she wants to complete college. Ask for help with an underlying problem that is causing the truancy.

I take great pains to choose my community representatives thoughtfully because I know the difference they can make. I want the community representative to be relevant. For example, if a homeless teen is the offender, I may want an adult that has overcome homelessness to sit in the circle to express empathy and understanding without condescending judgment, while still empowering the youth to be responsible for behaviors. I want a coach or teacher who can speak to a chronically disruptive student's strengths to sit in as a supporter and hold an overall balance of thought so that a blame game doesn't erupt. I want a former offender to act as a community representative when a similar behavior problem is at issue so he or she can give insight as to why such things occur.

The job of a community representative is to listen carefully to all sides, to be objective, and to hold the offender accountable. She should ask relevant questions about the incident and help decide what consequences best fit with the offense. He or she may end up telling a story of how a similar event affected life in the aftermath of a crime or offense. The community representative can speak honestly and openly and bring up issues that the others who may be too close to the issue may not think of or that are too sensitive for a particular person to introduce. The community representative can help move the conference to fruition by keeping things in perspective. Most importantly, the community representative must help the participants focus on repair—not punishment.

Set the Standard

Keep the standard high. Encourage your student facilitators to review the benefits of participating as leaders of the restorative justice process, such as resume building, work experience, reference letters from advisors, skill-building, and opportunities for leadership.

Set up a schedule for initial training and practice sessions for your boomerang team. Conduct multiple role-plays at each session. Use the sample role play from the Appendix or make one up of your own. Youth have a blast making up their own scenarios and taking turns playing the offender and victim roles.

It allows the facilitation team to bond and become a solid unit. Have the team study each of the tools provided in this book.

Talk about victim and offender mindsets in Appendix A and B. Provide some case studies that are relevant to the types of incidents you might see referred through the restorative justice conference. Use typical real life scenarios to which students can relate. Get testimonies from victims and offenders. Show and discuss a video; there are many great films available such as "Stand and Deliver"; "Freedom Writers"; or "The Ron Clark Story" as well as films specifically about restorative justice found on the Web. You might also have students read a few books such as those listed in Chapter 1, or perhaps *Touching Spirit Bear*.

Now decide who will facilitate and who will co-facilitate. Emphasize in your training with student facilitators that the facilitator will set the tone for the whole restorative justice experience. You want offenders and victims both to walk away with an experience of fairness. You want the victim to begin to feel safe again and to know that the offender was held accountable. Ideally, you want the offender to have listened with respect, not made excuses for him or herself, to have expressed genuine remorse and empathy for others, and to be willing to take an active role in repairing the harm that will lead to making better choices in the future. The facilitator can pave the way to this optimum outcome through an attitude and expression of genuine caring for each student, good eye contact, and mutual respect.

Reintegrative Shame Versus Stigmatizing Shame

Shame is translated: 'There's something wrong with me' rather than 'I did something wrong.' When we shame children, we offer them no way out.

~ H. Van Scoy, Ph.D

There is a vast difference between stigmatizing shame and reintegrative shame. One leaves a child hopeless, the other hopeful and more able to make amends.

~ John Braithwaite, New Zealand Criminologist

Shame is used as a tool of cruelty, and its victims often become cruel themselves.

~ David Hawkins (Power vs Force)

There is extraordinary wisdom in these three quotes. Distinguishing between the two types of shame defined by Braithwaite can take your results to greater heights. According to some accounts, we've come a long way from the days of Hester Prynne when 17th century Bostonians deeply shamed the adulteress by having her wear the scarlet letter "A" on her dress—a badge of shame. Led to the town's scaffold she is then publicly harangued. Hester may have gotten off easy. In colonial Maryland, the law provided for branding with hot irons: the initial "M" for murderer, "T" for thief, "R" for runaway slave and "H" for hog thief. We'd like to believe such practices no longer exist. But if we look carefully enough, the mechanism of shame is alive and well in the world today. Stigmatizing shame damages people. It sometimes assigns labels to our children that too easily leave an indelible imprint on their minds that, in turn, create insurmountable barriers to their self-discovery and destiny. Unlike the 17th century Puritans, we have enough information to put such shameful practices in the past and move toward more humane methods of behavior modification.

Now it's time for you to jump in feet first. Take a case. Produce some results on which you can debrief and give your boomerang team a chance to improve the process as you go. Help youth facilitators gain confidence as they build their skills. Once young offenders have completed their agreements, consider inviting them to become facilitators. Give them a chance to see the other side and take on a leadership role.

Chapter 4

Measure, Track, Evaluate

[Restorative justice] has been a financial boon. Discipline problems have all but disappeared. Out of 900 kids, we suspended only five this year.

~ Richard Hollahan, Assistant Principal
Newtown Middle School, Pennsylvania

Funders, whether individuals, corporate sponsors, charitable foundations or government sources, all want the biggest bang for their buck. They want to know what's in it for them. Is school and public safety a major concern to them? Will the results you anticipate be the ROI (return on investment) they're looking for? If the answer to those two questions is yes, then you've found your ideal partners. Community funders are often willing to provide support to one-time events, but in the case of a full-on implementation project, they want to know it will be sustainable in the coming years. And quite frankly, most don't want to be your only source of incubator funds.

To get funding support you will need to clearly demonstrate how you will define and measure success, and then, as your track record grows and proves viability, how you will gain additional local and state support (school, community, and government). If you are just now launching a restorative justice initiative in a school, a track record is probably out of the question. The good news is, other schools currently using restorative justice successfully may be able to provide some of that empirical data. Add their data to your case and you should be able to convince prospective supporters that the initiative has merit and will reduce discipline problems along with the need for suspension and expulsion—all while making your school community safer.

A Logic Model

On the opposite page is a customizable logic model that can help form the basis of your vision and help you measure progress.

Collect The Data

Following the logic model is a sample of additional data that can be collected specific to the restorative justice process and be integrated into your executive summary of results. The statistics you collected from step one involving academics, attendance, and behaviors can be added together with these to provide a solid foundation for a comprehensive evaluation.

RESTORATIVE JUSTICE LOGIC MODEL

Overall Objective:
Safe School Environment and Enhanced Academic Success

Goals	Targeted Groups	Activities
Improve school behavior, attendance and academic performance.	HS students with academic problems.	Individualized assessment and team review followed by monthly team review.
Improve school climate and safety.	High school students with behavior problems including truancy.	Restorative justice conferences to address school policy violation, incident of personal or property harm, or violation of the law. Youth and parents invited to attend.
Help youth develop effective decision-making skills.	Students returning to school after suspension, or short-term expulsion.	Urinalysis testing at the discretion of staff.
Increase resilience.		Summer school and behavior support program.
Foster positive relationships with adults and peers.		Social responsibility and character development training.
Facilitate succesful discharge from probation supervision (where appropriate).	Parents (guardians) of referred youth.	Data management.

Resources	Objectives	Performance Indicators
Teachers, counselors and administrators.	Reduced truancy and dropout rates.	School records indicate absences decreased 30% from previous semester.
Restorative justice curriculum.	Reduced need for suspension and expulsion.	Discipline referrals reduced 30%.
School resource officer(s).	Reduced recidivism and discipline referrals.	Suspensions and expulsions decreased 15%.
Family service agency.	Improved school climate and safety.	School climate survey demonstrates improved student and staff satisfaction.
Parents (guardians).	Improved academic performance.	GPAs improve .75 points on average from previous semester.
Evaluation staff.	Develop student mentoring program with students who complete.	Improved student attitudes—respect, listening skills, and anger control.
Third party researchers.	Celebration and recognition of achievements.	
Continued staff training.	Constructive correction of behavioral relapses.	
	Decreased criminal risk.	

RESTORATIVE JUSTICE CONFERENCE MEASUREMENTS

SAMPLE CASE REFERRALS AND OUTCOMES

Total separate cases processed	480
Number of offenders involved	521
Number of direct victims	428
Number of volunteer community participants	639
Number of offender supporters	1222
Number of victim supporters	1414
Number of cases returned to referral agency as incomplete	14
Success rate of Agreements completed	93%
Recidivism rate (% of individuals that re-offended)	8.6%
Satisfaction rate for offenders	94%
Satisfaction rate for impacted victims and community representatives	100%

STUDENT DEMOGRAPHICS

% Female student offenders	22%
% Male student offenders	78%
% Freshmen	13%
% Sophomores	35%
% Juniors	28%
% Seniors	24%

AGREEMENT ITEMS COMPLETED

Community service hours	1233
Anger management sessions	14
AA meetings attended	233
Written apologies made	125
Reflection/research papers	146
Safe school flyers or posters created	942

Chapter 5

Connect Your Community with Informal Circles

You cannot separate behavior from academics. When students feel good and safe and have solid relationships with teachers, their academic performance improves.

~ David Piperato, former principal
Palisades High School, Pennsylvania

Not Enough Time

One of the loudest outcries of teachers today is "not enough time"—not enough time to teach, to correct papers, to get kids to pass state testing, to check heads for lice, check backpacks for weapons, to censor tee shirt messages, wage war on drugs, and definitely no "extra" time to discipline. Yet discipline problems continue to plague schools, youth organizations, homes, the workplace, and yes, even our faith communities. Hope springs eternal in an ancient practice simply referred to as *circles*, now finding their way into schools to promote positive behaviors and culture shifts. They are the perfect complement to the formal restorative justice process. They provide teachers with a dynamic way to create beneficial community connectedness in the classroom.

We humans are great storytellers. We value stories. In fact, many of us have left profoundly important lectures and motivational seminars and the only thing we remember a week later is the story that one of the presenters told. Stories connect us. We relate to the storyteller's message oftentimes because we've had similar hardships, wonderments, or experiences of hilarious delight. Circle dialogs offer an ideal means to get our human stories out and open a path to understanding.

Our earliest ancestors knew instinctively that circle discussions provide a format that sends a powerful message; namely, there is no hierarchy here, we are all equally important, and we all can be leaders. When we are *in circle*, there are no barriers between us; we listen to one another; show respect for one another; and we value one another's thoughts and ideas. Most early indigenous peoples used a *talking instrument* that gave the speaker the chance to speak without interruption, while all others became committed listeners. Today we give descriptive names to circles: Talking Circles, Peacemaking Circles, Healing Circles, Circles of Understanding, Sentencing Circles, Planning Circles, Women's and Men's Circles. Virtually any kind of conversation or discussion can be held *in circle*. Circles are sacred places where genuine listening can heal the very soul of another human being.

Having worked with many thousands of young people over the past thirty plus years, I have seen a growing unfilled need in children today to be heard, particularly among those youth struggling with harsh socio-economic conditions or acutely dysfunctional families. A dear friend of mine grew up in Tanzania where he said children were not spoken to—they were not seen as having anything important to say. Having lived in America for several decades since, he now sees the vital importance of communicating with children and the contrast in a child's development when she is listened to with deep interest and respect.

When a teacher intuitively takes advantage of any opportunity to connect with students, it can have a lifelong impact. Circle discussions have been used to create profound culture shifts in high risk schools like West Philadelphia High School in Pennsylvania. On the state's "Persistently Dangerous Schools" list for six years, West Philadelphia High began to experience positive results in less than a year using restorative practices. Circles provide a missing link that can transition even dangerous war-torn environments such as this into safe schools. The more widely they are used in a school, the more likely a culture change will take root.

There are many ways to use circles. They can be used as icebreakers; to smooth out inevitable disagreements or discord; to ward off misunderstanding, anger or potential violence; or to build mutually rewarding relationships. Those relationships can be among students, between teachers and students, and between teachers and school administrators. When used effectively, circles are the entry point to having students take responsibility for and pride in their school. Joseph Roy, Principal of Springfield Township High School, Pennsylvania, says of the restorative circles model, "When you get to the point where it's informal but constant, that's where you want to be."

Unlike a formal restorative justice model that lends itself to specific incidents of harm to another human being, circles offer an informal way to build and deepen connection. As I mentioned previously in this book, it is *connection to community* that profoundly deters crime and re-offending.

The Talking Instrument

Before we get into a few exciting ideas on how you might use circles to your greatest advantage, let's circle up about talking instruments. A talking instrument helps to control the flow of conversation so that each person can speak without interruption. It is a great way to teach listening skills and respect for others. Circles are a great way to give youth who rarely speak a chance to do so, and others who often monopolize the conversation a chance to listen. Kids often self-regulate when one person seems to be talking too much and giving others little time to participate. You never want to force someone to speak. Set a guideline in the beginning that anyone who wishes to may pass. The typically silent ones, when given that freedom and flexibility, will soon join in as they hear the stories of others and see the inevitable openness that comes naturally from storytelling and from listening without ridicule or harsh judgment.

Using a talking piece with a symbolic or meaningful metaphor will help you set the tone you want to create for a specific topic of discussion. We often use a boomerang in our circles as it so beautifully conveys the message that what you give out comes back—anger comes back as anger, respect comes back as respect. Humorous as it may sound, we also use a fairy godmother magic wand. Older or gang affiliated youth generally balk or titter at the idea of such a seemingly silly talking piece at first, but it's always fun to watch even them choose the magic wand at a later time. It conveys the message that each of us is the magician of our own life. When we take charge of our lives and make positive choices, magic happens.

Another popular talking piece is the eagle feather. We quickly relate that an authentic eagle feather has been used for centuries by Native Americans, and only they have the legal right today to use one. Because it is illegal to kill one of these elegant and majestic endangered birds, even Native Americans must apply to a repository to obtain one of its body parts such as a feather, a process that could take months or years. For that reason, the faux eagle feather we use in our circles is a turkey feather painted to look like an eagle's.

Using the feather as a talking piece can be an outstanding opportunity to set a tone of reverence that will permeate the circle dialog and generate a deep appreciation for listening. Without realizing it, students' budding listening skills lead to empathy and compassion for others as well as for themselves. The facilitator's attitude about the circle will be starkly apparent in the way it gets mirrored by the group.

The use of a faux eagle feather could be a great opportunity to study the Native American culture and the significance of their circle traditions. We once invited Kaweah, a Native American woman leader, out to lead one of our adult training circles. She brought with her a real eagle feather adorned with intricate beading and leather work along the stem that was to be given as a birthday gift to her hundred-year-old grandmother. She helped us to understand the importance of the eagle feather to her people—that because the eagle flies the highest of all birds, it can take our words high up into the Heavens, and, thus, relies on us to speak only the truth. We did several "go-rounds" in the circle that day and were spellbound as people shared from depths that would not have been possible without Kaweah's reverent tone. By circle's end, the bonds were inseparable, and there wasn't a dry eye in the house.

Now, here are just a few ideas on how circles can lead to a positive culture change in your school. Some of you may say you don't have enough time to add circles to your already full plates. However, I urge you to stay open to the possibility of creating an environment where students look forward to a circle discussion even once a week that will give them a voice and allow them to be heard in a way many of them have never before experienced and perhaps never will again outside of school.

Check-ins and Check-outs

Circles are great barometers to test how students are responding to your lesson plans, to uncover barriers to learning, or simply to "take a pulse" on how kids are doing emotionally or mentally. Used as brief morning check-ins or late-in-the-day check-outs, circles can help you and your students get on the same page or see things in a new light. Can you ask these same questions in a lecture-style format with a teacher in front of the room and students behind their desks? Of course, but don't underestimate the magic of a circle to draw out discussions that will never come out of a lecture. Be prepared to have students blow you away with the profound depth of their verbal and emotional contributions. Watch as the classroom environment begins to subtly evolve from separateness to community.

These open-ended questions can kick off a great check-in or check-out:

- So how is everyone doing today? Is there anything going on for you that could be a barrier to your learning today?
- If you were the principal of this school, what is the first thing you would do to make things better?
- Describe the best possible school.
- Who has been your favorite teacher, and why? (This doesn't have to be a school teacher; it can be a relative, a friend, or employer.)
- What concerns do you have about the homework I assigned yesterday?

- You all heard our principal on this morning's announcements say there will be a community meeting to discuss whether some schools need to close due to serious budget cuts. How do you feel about that?
- Today's lesson was a tough one, but it will prepare each of you for the big test on Friday. Can you think of any reason why each of you won't get an A on that test?
- How can we get creative and find a way to help each and every person get an A on Friday's test? Let's hear your ideas.
- Yesterday there was a fight on the school grounds and several students were badly hurt and were taken away in an ambulance. Does anyone wish to talk about that this morning?
- What was the most valuable thing you learned this week? (It doesn't have to be something they learned at school.)

If you're still thinking there isn't enough time for a "check-in," that may be the very day a student has a real need for support from peers or teachers. Not addressed, it easily could result in a distracted student, strained tension within the group, or even negative acting out. Setting a routine day of the week or time of day for check-ins creates a delicious anticipation as students begin to look forward to their chance to be heard.

Start of the School Year

Each year students leave the summer behind and come to school with certain expectations—some with reluctance, others with boundless enthusiasm. As an enlightened teacher, you naturally want to funnel this mixed energy toward your own expectations. Starting the year off with a circle process, whether you choose daily, weekly, or once a month or "as needed" circles, can help you bring students around to your way of thinking more quickly and enrich their classroom experience (and yours). Circles help you build instant rapport, and they help students shake off any residual anxiety from the previous years' frustrating battles or fears of failure. When they know you care, they will unconsciously find themselves caring about you as well as their fellow classmates. Setting that tone up front is critical to the success of your circles.

Because circles have the power to transform lives, they must be used judiciously and with great care as a vehicle for each student's personal growth. Watch throughout the year as your youth grow in confidence, learn to speak more easily before a group, and more eloquently articulate their thoughts.

Here are some great questions that can pave the way to that all important start-of-the-year classroom bonding.

- What was the most difficult thing you've ever had to overcome (yesterday, this summer, or in your life)?
- If you could be guaranteed 100% success this year at school, what would that look like?
- What would you do with a million dollars?
- What movie best describes your life?
- What actor/actress would you want to play the role of you in a movie?
- If you were to receive a 30-day, all-expenses paid vacation to anywhere in the world, where would you go and who would you take?
- Describe one person in your life who has had the most positive influence on you and tell us why.
- If you could choose the perfect career designed just for you and know that you would be successful at it, what would it be?

A word of caution from years of experience: as the facilitator, simply say a heartfelt "thank you" after each person has spoken—an acknowledgement for their willingness to participate. Avoid singling out participants with value judgments such as "great job" or "that's awful." It is deflating to those who don't get praised, and shuts down those who fear upcoming disparaging remarks.

Circles to Address Behavior Problems

Restorative circles are not for wimps. They can address behavior problems with extraordinary power when facilitated with objectivity and a straightforward Socratic approach. There are enough behavior problems in schools to be able to select relevant questions that provide rich discussion material that affects everyone. It helps to bring out into the open issues that otherwise are swept under the rug or remain unresolved or left to fester beneath the surface. Here are some examples.

- If you've ever been a victim of theft (or had something stolen from you), how did that feel and how did you respond?
- How would you feel if your locker was vandalized and the money you were saving to buy medication for a family member was taken?
- What do you think a teacher should do if her purse is stolen from out of her desk?
- How does gossip affect a school?
- What would you like to say about gang violence?
- What consequence should there be for someone who shouts racial slurs at another person?
- In your opinion does suspension or expulsion work?
- What are some ideas you may have that could be more effective than detention?
- Who does painting graffiti on school or neighborhood property hurt and who has to pay to repair the damage?
- If someone came onto school property and tried to sell drugs to your little sister or brother, how would you feel?
- How would you define alcohol abuse?
- What are some of the reasons kids join gangs?

If these sorts of questions scare the living daylights out of you or cause you to fear kids' responses, keep in mind that these are the very issues many kids are thinking about when they come to class. These are the kinds of thoughts that, hidden from view, can put up walls to learning. The open-minded teacher who is ready to listen without judgment may be pleasantly surprised when students begin to "coach" one another in how to overcome addictions and bad behaviors simply because it's out in the open. A teacher does not have to act as a social worker or psychologist in these circles. As the circle facilitator, he or she has the unique opportunity to "sit back" and watch where the conversation goes and let the kids counsel one another. It can be quite liberating.

I vividly recall an experience at an alternative high school during one of our signature teen *Boomerang* workshops (a motivational, character development and social responsibility training). These were students that generally had dropped out of or were expelled from public schools, yet, to their credit, saw the value of returning to get a high school diploma. On the first day of the training, as always, we helped students build a big dream for their lives, one that would inspire them to stay in school and take simple steps to reach their short- and long-term goals. These, like so many other youths, were aspiring paramedics, NFL football players, chefs, tattoo artists, and famous rap stars. Now that we had their attention, on the second day of our three-day training we were able to ask our usual series of questions that would help students reveal some difficult trials or traumas they may have undergone. For example, we asked them to please stand up if they had ever been lonely; if they'd ever been ridiculed by a teacher; if they'd ever lost a friend or loved one to gang or domestic violence, or to suicide. The energy in the room became heavy as a few students voluntarily related stories of friends who were shot or who died in their arms after a violent gang war; another who spoke of being beaten repeatedly by her step-father to the point of unconsciousness; and yet another who had been brutally kicked in the stomach and miscarried her baby. As the stories unfolded, several of the teens began crying.

When the session ended, the youth quietly filed out of the room, some arm in arm, to return to their separate classrooms. The school counselor came up to us, frantically voicing that she would now need to bring in additional social service resources to help the youth overcome their emotional trauma from the discussion. As it turned out, it was not necessary. Instead, following the third day's session, evaluations were passed out to students. In the blank space requesting what "the best part" of the training was, consistent answers showed students valued being able to talk about their bottled up issues most. Many of those same students returned to subsequent workshops to tell new students about their moment of epiphany experienced in the workshop and how that chance to self-express released pent-up emotions, freeing them to discover a support system in their peers. They began to help one another focus on a positive future. It gave the teen that had been beaten by her step-father the courage to go home and tell him he could never do that again. She proudly reported even a year later that after that day, she and her dad experienced a true father-daughter relationship built on respect. Countless *Uptalk* graduates became leaders after that and were catalysts for a dramatically improved energy in the entire school.

Creative Formats for Circles

There are a number of formats to use to enhance circle discussions:

SINGLE CIRCLE: A single circle of chairs, one for each participant, is the most common. So long as there is adequate space, the single circle of chairs lends itself to that strong message of equality and ensures each person is clearly visible to the entire group.

DOUBLE CIRCLE: If the room is too small or the size of the group too large for a single circle, consider a double circle, sometimes referred to as a "coliseum." This format works particularly well in meetings where the primary speakers are given seats in the inner circle, and those who are there essentially to listen are seated in the outer circle.

EMPTY CHAIR CIRCLE: This is an offshoot of the double circle, but one chair in the inner group of chairs is left empty. Depending on the intent of the circle, individuals from the outer circle may quietly take their place in the empty chair to await an appropriate moment to respond to a certain question. It is a chance for them to add their voice of concern about an issue, or ask a new question to the group. This is an effective means for brainstorming in a large group. For example teachers may want to use this to help a new teacher with ideas on how to deal with a particular student that is unresponsive or chronically disruptive. It is most effective when there is no critique of the suggested ideas, just a chance for the person receiving the ideas to capture and consider them.

LEADERSHIP CIRCLE: To instill leadership skills in your students, you might ask a different student each time to lead and facilitate the circle. If there are not enough circle opportunities to ensure that each student in your class will have that chance in the course of a year for instance, consider a lottery-type drawing pulling names from a hat. It can also be used to promote the leadership opportunity as a special honor. For those who get immobilized from stage fright, have several open-ended question ideas available for them to choose from, or give them enough lead time to think of one.

NON-SEQUENTIAL: Use a nerf ball as the talking piece and have students throw it randomly across the circle to the next speaker. You might start with a question such as, When are you feeling the most un-stressed?

CIRCLES FOR RITUALS: There may be occasions when a celebration is in order, where a single question by itself doesn't fulfill the purpose of the circle. For rituals or circle celebrations there are four natural parts to a circle: the opening; the question; the discussion; and the closing. Each provides an opportunity to meet the intent of the gathering and graciously acknowledge and honor each participant. An opening may consist of a student reading a carefully selected and relevant quote or gently striking a "singing bowl" from India. Next comes the open-ended question and discussion such as, What are you most proud of having accomplished this year? And, finally, the closing might include an original song sung by a talented student who wrote it just for this special occasion, or a song played from a CD that reinforces the intended message of the overall event.

CIRCLE OF HOPE: Whether a student has made an embarrassing blunder or a serious mistake that resulted in suspension, consider this transformative circle of hope as a way to transition them back to community. The embarrassed or offending student is asked to sit in a chair at the center, all others seated in the chairs around the circle. The facilitator asks each person in the circle to say one positive thing about the person in the center. Students being singled out in this way sometimes move reluctantly to the "hot seat" thinking they are going to be chastised. But have a box of tissues handy for tears that may flow when he or she begins to hear from peers about how certain helpful words, actions or befriending made a difference for others. Even in cases where this person has caused considerable harm to others, you may witness defensiveness transform to humility or gratitude. We used this "circle of hope" with enormous success when a particular "class clown" continually disrupted the flow of a workshop to get attention. Giving the student positive attention rather than negative provided an unfamiliar jolt and left the student speechless. There was marked improvement in his behavior after that.

Young people love ritual so long as it is meaningful and brings purpose to the circle. The circle separates the day from other routine activities. It builds community and offers a sense of stability as well as an expectation for meaningful camaraderie that breaks down emotional walls and builds stronger relationships.

A note about length of time for circles: It is wise to set a time limit for some types of circles. For example, when we know we have a particularly lively group that is having a hard time listening or getting focused, we've begun a workshop with, "We have some great things to share with you today, but first, for the next five minutes, you can talk about any topic you'd like. Then we'll move to the day's lessons." When we say "anything", we mean it, but we also hold a high standard for "appropriate" language—no cussing, and nothing off-color, or demeaning to others. Sometimes we give them some topics such as: gangs, drugs, prison, schoolwork, marriage, or even pre-marital sex. We don't add our comments to the discussion but let the youth take it where they want to go. Then, at the end of five minutes, we look at the clock and keep our promise to move on. This seems to release the pent up energy of most students and because we've listened with genuine interest and without judgment, they are more ready to listen to us. Keeping our promise to cut the discussion at the agreed upon time also gives us credibility and builds trust. Just as importantly, it ensures that anyone that has not yet had a chance to speak doesn't feel cut off or short-changed when the time is up.

What is the difference between the best teachers and the worst teachers? We often ask this question to the youth we serve. Their eyes light up as they describe the teachers they remember with fondness—those who create healthy limits and a high standard while providing sincere encouragement, resources, and support. They are the ones who know how to engage students, get them involved, and listen to their input. They are committed to the personal development of each student. A dedicated and truly enlightened teacher reaches us at a core level, may expect more of us than we do of ourselves, and helps us to stretch up to our potential. They work "with" us to help us grow and become independent, healthy human beings. The student who can easily recall such a teacher well into adulthood is fortunate indeed.

Here are a few more great ideas that have been contributed by students and teachers on how to use circles:

- Circle of welcome for a new student in the classroom
- Circle of diversity and respect (appreciation for ethnicity, culture, the elderly, handicapped, etc.)
- Circle for gift giving
- Preparation for a field trip or an event (to set guidelines and expectations)
- Develop a mission statement for class
- Reflection time (What was one important point in today's assignment?)
- Training of student leaders
- Circle of attitude or attitude adjustment
- Response to a relevant proverb or quote
- Review of lessons
- Circle of solutions to a problem
- Circle of peace
- To diminish racial or gang tension
- To hear a guest speak
- To invite a victim of a crime to talk about healing and recovery
- To discuss community responsibility
- To set life intentions

Chapter 6

Final Thoughts

When one door of happiness closes, another opens; but often we look so long at the closed door that we do not see the one which has been opened for us.

~ Helen Keller

Restorative Justice: A Doorway to Discipline

My grandparents lived in an age when the world was changing at a rapid pace. Every twenty years of so, life was completely different than it was two decades earlier. Today, our children are experiencing warp speed as technology changes nearly everything about the way we live every five years. How do we help our children keep up? As we prepare our children for the 21st century and beyond, let us take heed of prophetic messages from the futurists—those who scientifically study trends to predict the future. It is their belief that adults of tomorrow will, in fact, not keep up unless they have good critical thinking skills.

Let's say you were a CEO of a small company that provides sports equipment and clothing through its fifteen regional retail outlets. Your company has remained viable even in tough economic times because you always try to hire the right people with the right attitudes who will remain loyal. What skills do you want in your new hires? Outside of on-the-job training, what are the most important skills or areas of knowledge that you will base your selection on from the following list?

- Algebra
- Biology
- Chemistry

- Social Skills/People Skills
- Teambuilding Skills
- English Grammar
- Oral/Speaking Skills
- Conflict Resolution Skills
- Basic Math
- Economics and Financial Literacy
- Critical Thinking Skills
- Emotional Stability and Coping Skills
- Problem Solving
- Information Literacy, Communication Skills (ability to access, evaluate, and use information and communicate it to others)
- Science
- U.S. History
- Foreign Language
- Technology (ability to use today's technological resources)

This brief exercise opened my eyes just a little wider as I contemplated what our schools of the future will need to be teaching. It is human nature to hold onto the familiar. But as George Lucas would tell us, the concept of schools was invented during the Agricultural Age when children needed to be available to work in the fields during the planting and harvest seasons. Then came the Industrial Age where able bodies had to learn to work long hours in factories. Schools were places of indoctrination where information was presented as truth, and students were expected to memorize and accept the data as fact.

Today, in order for our children to compete in the workforce, they must be better prepared to think for themselves, take advantage of technological advances and resources, and they must be better able to interrelate with us and with one another. Restorative justice and restorative practices clearly are foundational elements that can enhance that journey. They are a doorway to discipline that can open up to a rich connectedness of spirit in our homes, our communities, and in our schools. An exciting door has opened for us. It's up to each of us to walk through it.

Appendix A

Offender
States of Mind

TRAINING TOOL FOR YOUR
BOOMERANG TEAM TRAINING

Those who cause harm sometimes avoid taking responsibility for their behaviors through these skewed states of mind:

Physical

- I have bruises, broken bones, cuts, burns, scars, black eyes, lost teeth.
- I have stomach aches and pains.
- I was raped and am pregnant with a child I didn't plan for.
- I was raped and now I have a sexually transmitted disease.
- I have an ulcer.
- I am always tired. My energy is drained away.

Emotional

- I am afraid.
- I am angry.
- I feel hopeless and helpless.
- I feel insecure and isolated.
- I am sad. I feel like crying all the time.
- I feel guilty, like I must be to blame for this.
- I feel so ashamed and embarrassed.
- I am confused, depressed, and sometimes feel suicidal.
- I feel vulnerable and powerless.

Psychological

- I'm paranoid of others and of being alone.
- I feel intimidated by people.
- I have constant crying outbursts.
- I'm unable to sleep.
- I feel so unclean. I want to bathe or wash many times a day.
- I'm depressed and I want to die.
- I have nightmares.
- I can't have a normal, healthy sexual relationship with my spouse now.

Financial

- I have to pay for the damages of this crime that I didn't ask for, and now I can't pay my rent.
- I lost time from work and didn't get paid for the time I was out.
- I lost my job because I was so traumatized by the crime.
- It cost me a lot of money to go to court and pay a lawyer to defend myself against the person who committed this offense against me.
- I have medical costs.
- I have funeral costs to bury my loved one.

In the conventional system victims rarely have a say in how the harm will be repaired. In a restorative system, victims have a chance to be heard and take an active role in the process to get questions answered, to help decide consequences, and begin to feel safe again.

Appendix B

Offender Thinking Errors

TRAINING TOOL FOR YOUR
BOOMERANG TEAM TRAINING

Those who cause harm sometimes experience thinking errors:

Entitlement/Privilege

- I'm special. I deserve special consideration.
- I can do anything I want; my father's name is on a building here.
- I (or my parents) will just pay for it.
- I already paid my dues in life. I can take what I want.
- I'm above the law. The law doesn't apply to me.
- I have the right to steal when I need something. "They" won't miss it; they have plenty more where that came from.
- Society owes me.
- It's okay to be irresponsible once in a while.
- It's all in fun. Where's your sense of humor?

Justification

- Everyone else is doing it. Why shouldn't I?
- My life is hard. Society is to blame for that.
- The victim had it coming.
- I didn't physically harm anyone, so it's no big deal.
- If I hadn't done it, someone else would have.

False Power

- I have authority issues. I don't want anyone telling me what to do.
- If someone disrespects me, I have to straighten them out.
- I want to be the one in control.
- I have to pay back people who mess with me.
- There's only one way for me to protect myself—fight.

Criminal Rationalization

- Anything can be fixed in court if you have enough money or the right connections.
- Bankers, lawyers, and politicians get away with breaking the law, so why shouldn't I?
- A plea bargain is a lie; so who cares if I lie?
- Police do worse things than the criminals do, so it's us against them.

Personal Irresponsbility

- I only went to prison because of bad luck.
- The real reason I'm in prison is because of the color of my skin.
- I'm not to blame for anything I've done.
- Laws are just a way to keep poor people down.
- I'm a criminal; but my environment and upbringing made me that way. I had no choice.

Appendix C

Sample Role Plays

TRAINING TOOL FOR YOUR
BOOMERANG TEAM TRAINING

Use these two sample role plays as templates, and have your boomerang team create their own scenarios that relate to typical incidents found at your school. Cut up the separate roles and hand them out to students learning to facilitate.

ROLE PLAY NUMBER ONE:
POSSESSION OF A KNIFE

GENERAL INFORMATION: Brian is a 15-year-old boy. He lives with his mother and two younger brothers. Brian recently brought a switchblade knife to school. The school and family agreed to hold a restorative justice conference about the incident.

NUMBER OF ROLES: Five or six including facilitator

Facilitator
As facilitator of the RJ conference, your role is to ensure the safety of participants and to set a tone of respect. You want people to speak honestly and emotionally, but without any chance for re-victimization or out-of-control volatility. Read the restorative justice script verbatim (found in Chapter Three of this book).

Mrs. Tracy - Mother Of The Person Who Caused Harm

Your son Brian is a fifteen-year-old boy. He lives with you and his two younger brothers. You work as a receptionist at a nearby office. Brian recently brought a switchblade knife to school and was suspended. The school and family agreed to hold a restorative justice conference about the incident.

You believe Brian has a job at a local supermarket. You are very proud of him and thankful for all the help he gives you. Recently Brian brought home a large TV and a microwave, and he helps you out by buying some of his brothers' school clothes and supplies. He also stays home with the younger boys when they're sick so you can work.

You don't think his having the knife at school was such a big deal. You feel the school set him up so they can transfer him to a school for troubled youth. You believe the teachers resent a hard-working, enterprising youth like your Brian.

Brian - Person Who Caused Harm

You are a 15-year-old boy. You live with your mother and your two younger brothers. You recently brought a switchblade knife to school. The school and family agreed to hold a restorative justice conference about the incident. You're not anxious to go to the conference, but you don't want to get expelled from school either (which would be your only alternative).

You have had erratic school attendance for several years, and sometimes you stay home to take care of younger brothers when they are sick so your mom can work. You know she doesn't make much money and you know she works hard so you try to help out when the family needs something. You've been shoplifting and stealing purses for almost a year now but your mother thinks you've got a job at a local supermarket. You recently brought home a large TV and a microwave. Sometimes you buy your brothers' clothes and school supplies.

Some kids were showing you disrespect at school, so you got the switchblade knife from a friend and took it to school to stop their ridicule and name-calling. You don't think it was a big deal, but the school staff are getting real tough about it. You are a little upset with the teacher who told on you because you thought she liked you, so now you feel betrayed.

As the conference progresses, your conscience begins to bother you. When the police officer begins to ask what supermarket you're working at, you admit that you don't work for any; that you've been shoplifting and stealing money from purses.

Vice Principal Milligan, Person Who Was Harmed
Your job is to keep the school safe, yet you feel that the incident of Brian bringing the knife to school has put other students in danger. If he had gotten into a fight, someone could have been seriously hurt. You are angry that Brian would even consider bringing the knife to school without any thought of the potential harm or consequences. Although you are willing to give the conference a try as a last resort, you feel it will take a lot of remorse and attitude turnaround not to expel Brian. And, if the conference doesn't work, you are thinking of instituting immediate expulsion for similar incidents.

Teacher Ms. Jung - Person Who Was Harmed
You were the first adult to see Brian with the switchblade knife when he was showing it off to another youth in the hallway. Brian was one of your students last year and you've always liked him but now you are afraid of him. You knew he was having some problems with absenteeism and suspected there might be some issues troubling him at home or in his personal life, but didn't really know how to help. When you used to ask him about it, he wouldn't give you an answer. Now he avoids answering those sorts of questions. At this point your concern is that the school environment is becoming less and less safe for students and for staff. You are thinking of quitting your job because of this incident.

School Police Officer Anderson
You are not happy about having to come to the conference because you think that kids with knives and guns shouldn't

be tolerated in schools and should be sent to juvenile facilities where they can't harm anyone. You are very upset to have heard that the teacher Ms. Jung is actually thinking about quitting her job because of Brian's careless behavior in bringing the switchblade knife to school. You ask what supermarket Brian works for because you want to be sure he does not bring the switchblade to work with him. You are ready to speak to his employer at the supermarket because you know each of them in the neighborhoods personally.

ROLE PLAY NUMBER TWO: DISRESPECTFUL STUDENT

GENERAL INFORMATION: A junior high school student is constantly interrupting class by side-talking with his friends, making flippant comments to the teacher when called upon, and gets other kids in trouble when they get involved in the disruptive behaviors. The teacher has been making unsuccessful attempts to stop the behaviors and has now sent the boy to the assistant principal's office. They agreed to try conferencing before considering a two-day suspension.

NUMBER OF ROLES: Six including the facilitator

Facilitator
As facilitator of the Conference, your role is to ensure the safety of participants and to set a tone of respect. You want people to speak honestly and emotionally, but without any chance for re-victimization or out-of-control volatility. Read the restorative justice script verbatim (found in Chapter Three of this book).

Jerroll, Person Who Caused Harm
It doesn't take much effort on your part to get B's and C's, but you are more interested in socializing in school than doing your work. Your math teacher is demanding and rarely smiles. You frequently distract your classmates by talking and making jokes when the teacher asks questions, or you sometimes make faces when the teacher turns her back. You love it when you get a good laugh.

This past week, however, your teacher sent you to the assistant principal's office after she asked you a number of times not to talk during class or make jokes when she asks you questions. You know she has documented your behaviors, and now you face a two-day school suspension. You had heard about the conferencing program and asked the assistant principal if you could do that instead. You genuinely want to know why your behavior is such a problem when all you want to do is make a boring subject more interesting, and get the teacher Mrs. Blonder to lighten up.

Mrs. Blonder, Algebra Teacher

You are a junior high school math teacher. Jerroll is in your class. Since the very first day of class he has been disruptive and made jokes when called upon in class. You have addressed his disruptive behaviors several times in class and then twice more one-on-one after class, but the behavior has continued. You know that several of the students find Jerroll's disruptions humorous, but you feel it is disrespectful and that it has made it more difficult for students who don't find the subject as easy to grasp to remain focused and able to do their work.

The last time you spoke to Jerroll you warned him that you would send him to the assistant principal's office the next time an incident occurred, so when he got the whole class laughing at another student's wrong answer, you followed through on your warning.

You think he's probably a good kid, but he could be doing much better in math if he applied himself. You take your job seriously and want to see your students do well so that they will have valuable skills for the future. You know the state testing is coming up in a month and you feel that a number of the students are way behind in their work and understanding of the concepts they will need to pass the tests.

Mr. Westly, Assistant Principal

This is not the first time you have spoken to Jerroll this school year. Other teachers also have mentioned behavior problems, even though they haven't sent him to your office. You hate to use suspension for classroom behavior management, but you can't allow the disrespect to continue. You talked to Mrs. Blonder about conferencing as an alternative since Jerroll seemed to be willing to resolve the issue.

Joe, Jerroll's Friend

You were in math class when Jerroll was sent to the office. You like Jerroll because he's fun and you like being around him. But, you think he's gone too far in Mrs. Blonder's class. You think Mrs. Blonder is pretty up-tight, but math is pretty hard for you and you think maybe Mrs. Blonder just wants to be sure everyone gets the math skills they need. You want to support Jerroll, but you hope he'll stop horsing around so you can pay attention. You don't want him to think you're being disloyal to him as a friend by saying these things; but you feel like you'll get your parents upset if you don't do well in this class. You are afraid you'll flunk the state testing because you just don't understand algebra concepts.

Francine, A Fellow Student

You are a student at the same school but in a different math class with Mrs. Blonder. You have had the opportunity to facilitate conferences with students, but this is your first time being in a restorative justice conference with a teacher. You think Mrs. Blonder is a very smart person and you're learning a lot in her class. You also think that Jerroll is cute and you've had fun hanging out with him and his friends. You want to be fair and objective to both Jerroll and Mrs. Blonder.

Appendix D

Case Study

**TRAINING TOOL FOR YOUR
BOOMERANG TEAM TRAINING**

Eddie, a heavy-set middle school student in the eighth grade, was a well-known bully. He deeply disliked one of the seventh graders, William, who was a thin-built track star. One day both boys were lined up for a fire drill outside the school. Rain clouds were beginning to move in, so William took it upon himself to round up his classmates to go back inside after the fire drill was ended. Yelling over the crowd, he directed his fellow students to line up single file. Eddie shouted "Loser!" at him, and William turned and gave Eddie a dirty look, but kept yelling to his classmates. As William turned to walk toward the school, Eddie casually put his foot out and tripped William, but pretended to lose his balance and fell directly on top of the boy, intentionally crushing the wind out of him.

Unable to move, William began to cry, which made Eddie laugh out loud. Their classmates watched in horror as William raised his head and blood sprayed out of his nose and mouth, one of his front teeth now missing. An avalanche of screaming students alerted one of the teachers who arrived just in time to see Eddie helping William to his feet.

How would you handle this case in a restorative manner? What would be the optimum outcome? Who would you invite to participate in the restorative justice conference? Would the consequences of Eddie's actions go beyond the restorative process and result in suspension, expulsion, or assault charges by police? How would you feel if you were Eddie's parents? William's parents? What if William had a concussion as the result of the impact on the cement sidewalk? Would that change your approach? What if there were hospital and doctor bills to pay—who should pay them? How might you address William's problem with bullying? Could this incident result in a higher level of awareness in the school for the dangers of bullying? What restorative response could help both Eddie and William?

Appendix E

Needs and Feelings

TRAINING TOOL FOR
YOUR BOOMERANG TEAM TRAINING

Frequently youth (and adults) get confused between needs and feelings. Having your student facilitators familiarize themselves with the lists of words below will allow them to help other students articulate their needs and separate them from their feelings.

I Feel...

POSITIVE	NEGATIVE
Appreciated	Abandoned
Accepted	Angry
Admired	Afraid
Confident	Alienated
Calm	Alone
Content	Annoyed
Comfortable	Anxious
Cared about	Antagonistic
Caring	Arrogant
Excited	Ashamed
Ecstatic	Bad
Elated	Belittled

Encouraged	Bitter
Enthusiastic	Bored
Excited	Bothered
Fortunate	Cautious
Grateful	Confused
Hopeful	Controlled
Important	Cynical/Skeptical
Included	Defeated
Inspired	Degraded
Interested	Dejected
Needed	Depressed
Optimistic	Desperate
Patient	Disappointed
Peaceful	Discouraged
Pleased	Disgusted
Powerful	Disliked
Proud	Dissatisfied
Relaxed	Disturbed
Respected	Embarrassed
Safe	Emotional
Supported	Frantic
Surprised	Frustrated
Thankful	Furious
Understood	Guilty
Worthy	Helpless
	Lonely
	Manipulated
	Resentful
	Sad
	Self-conscious
	Shocked
	Trapped
	Used
	Worthless

The great work of Marshall Rosenberg (*Non-Violent Communication*) is one more important facet to the overall social-emotional intelligence paradigm. Rosenberg emphasizes that most conflict can be diffused or averted when we are clear about what we actually need. But, oftentimes, we're unaware of what our needs are. When given a list of needs such as those below, we can begin to identify those needs and ask for help in getting them met.

I Need...

Acceptance	Appreciation	Authenticity
Autonomy	Awareness	Beauty
Celebration	Challenge	Clarity
Community	Connection	Consideration
Contribution	Cooperation	Creativity
Effectiveness	Empathy	Enjoyment
Equality	Exploration	Freedom
Growth	Harmony	Honesty
Humor	Imagination	Inclusion
Inspiration	Integrity	Joy
Kindness	Learning	Love
Meaning	Movement	Order
Participation	Peace	Play
Presence	Protection	Respect
Rest	Safety & Health	Self-Expression
Spontaneity	Support	Touch
Trust	Truth	Understanding

Appendix F

Additional Ideas for Launching a Restorative Justice Initiative

More great ideas for launching, promoting, or celebrating your restorative justice initiative from enthusiastic restorative justice practitioners:

- Plan a surprise lunch for your action team to celebrate the completion of your first real-life restorative justice conference.
- Give award certificates to facilitators.
- Buy boomerang tee shirts from www.YouthTransformationCenter.org for your team.
- Provide youth facilitators with a letter of recommendation for their college portfolio.
- Recruit new advocates.
- Train and mentor new youth facilitators.
- When you have no more discipline problems at your school, send youth facilitators to the other feeder schools to help implement the process and transform the lives of more youth.
- Make your success stats available to the general public, on your school website, or in education digests.
- Report your findings and results to the National PTA.
- Encourage the use of restorative justice in the workplace, in youth detention centers, and in faith communities.
- Partner with feeder schools and the district.

- Sing your own praises.
- Write a press release and get your school some positive media coverage.
- Write an article for your school newsletter.
- Get recognized by your Department of Education.
- Go after a grant or have your school district apply for one.
- Get a corporate or business sponsor.
- Have the restorative justice youth facilitators give a presentation at the school assembly.
- Hire a full-time restorative justice coordinator at your school.
- Have the youth restorative justice boomerang team design flyers or posters and post them around the school.
- Declare a restorative justice day and plan an awareness event around it.
- Give an exceptional volunteer community member a "volunteer of the year" award in front of the school assembly, or at a community business luncheon.

About the Author

Jeannette Holtham

A veteran youth and adult leadership trainer, Jeannette Holtham is founder and president of the Youth Transformation Center in Denver, Colorado. Holtham has facilitated scores of restorative justice conferences and helped train both primary and secondary school educators, school resource officers, university professors, prison and youth detention center staff, police officers, district attorneys, and probation officers in the restorative justice philosophy and conferencing model. She instills her passion and commitment into her lifelong vision that all children should have at least one positive adult role model to nurture their spirits and inspire them on their way to adulthood.

Visit the Youth Transformation Center online at
YouthTransformationCenter.org.

The global restorative justice movement is here to stay. Around the world, even the most dangerous, high-risk schools are reducing discipline problems by up to sixty percent. Complementing your current school discipline practices with this simple, step-by-step restorative justice model will help you reach youth on a core level at a critical time in their young lives, when it's still possible to stop and reverse negative or destructive behavior.

CPSIA information can be obtained at www.ICGtesting.com
Printed in the USA
LVOW05s0550150314

377527LV00013B/62/P